Adaptive Technology
for
Special Human Needs

SUNY Series, Computers in Education
Cleborne D. Maddux, editor

Adaptive Technology
for
Special Human Needs

Arlene Brett and Eugene F. Provenzo, Jr.

State University of New York Press

ed by
York Press, Albany

© *1995 State University of New York*

For information, address State University of New York Press, State University Plaza, Albany, N.Y. 12246

Production by Dana Foote
Marketing by Theresa Abad Swierzowski

Library of Congress Cataloging-in-Publication Data

Brett, Arlene.
  Adaptive technology for special human needs / Arlene Brett and
Eugene F. Provenzo, Jr.
    p. cm. — (SUNY series, computers in education)
  Includes bibliographical references and index.
  ISBN 0–7914–2307–7 (hardcover : acid-free paper) — ISBN
0–7914–2308–5 (pbk. : acid-free paper).
    1. Special education—United States—Computer-assisted
instruction. 2. Handicapped—Education—United States—Computer
-assisted instruction. I. Provenzo, Eugene F. II. Title.
III. Series: SUNY series in computers in education.
LC3969.5.B74 1995
371.9'0285—dc20   94–17216
                                                              CIP

10 9 8 7 6 5 4 3 2 1

CONTENTS

_____

PREFACE

This is a book about how adaptive technology is changing the lives and learning of people with special needs. It attempts to provide the reader with a clear understanding of the possibilities and limitations inherent in this new field. In addition to providing a general overview of how computers can augment our functions as individuals, this work goes on to describe some of the major technologies available to people who have different types of disabilities.

Throughout the chapters included in this work, we refer to currently available hardware and software systems. These references are meant to provide general models and examples for the reader. Adaptive technology—like the computer field in general—is rapidly changing and evolving. New innovations are constantly developing that are redefining the field. While we hope to periodically update this work, we suggest that our readers will find it useful to pay attention not only to current computer magazines, but also to research journals dealing with computers and special education. Local school systems that have special education support centers, as well as university research special education centers are good sources of information for those interested in keeping up with the latest advances in technology. Organizations such as Closing the Gap (a national group which sponsors publications and conferences on adaptive technology) and TRACE Research and Development Center (a national clearinghouse for adaptive technology) are helpful sources of information for those interested in keeping current in the field. Finally, computer manufacturers such as Apple and IBM, as well as software companies, provide important sources of support and information for those interested in this new and exciting field.

To assist those readers interested in obtaining additional information about adaptive technology we have included three appendices at the conclusion of this work. Appendix A provides a list of manufacturers and distributors, Appendix B a list of information services and data bases, and Appendix C a list of organizations.

Many people have contributed to the development of this book. Particular thanks go to our case study participants who shared their lives and experiences with us: Catherine Garcia, John Paul Jebian, Lauren Matur, Mike Morgan, and Carrie Seigenthaler. Victoria Sartorio, Learning Resource Specialist at the Florida Diagnostic and Learning Resources System in Collier County, Florida, and Razia Pullen, her counterpart in Broward County were invaluable in helping us arrange interviews and providing us with information on new technologies. Edie Sloane of the Florida Diagnostic and Learning Resources System in Dade County Florida provided us with useful suggestions and assistance. Beth Saunders and Carol Farrell, both speech pathologists in the Broward County Schools, helped us with information and in arranging interviews. Stephanie Leighton of the Microcomputer Education for the Employment of the Disabled program (MEED) housed at Miami Dade Community College also provided us with important help. Nina Kasper, Preschool Varying Exceptionalities Teacher at Colonial Drive Elementary School in Miami gave us particularly valuable insights into the use of adaptive technology by teachers in early childhood settings.

Particular thanks go to Cristi Mitchell at Miami Dade Community College. Cristi assisted as a co-researcher on the development of the case studies included in this book. Together we share in the authorship of these case studies.

Finally, special thanks go to Asterie Baker Provenzo for her sage advice and consummate editorial skills.

1

INTRODUCTION

In November of 1990 Richard Ruopp, the former president of Bank Street College in New York City, gave a speech at an education conference sponsored by Columbia University without speaking a word. Ruopp has amyotrophic lateral sclerosis (loss of motor neurons resulting in the progressive loss of motor function), more commonly known as Lou Gehrig's disease. Despite having completely lost the ability to speak, Ruopp, with the help of a laptop computer, a software package called HandiChat Deluxe, and a DECtalk speech synthesizer, was able to give his presentation. Using this system, his speech, which had previously been typed into the computer, was "spoken" by the speech synthesizer. After completing his talk, Ruopp was able to answer questions from the audience by typing his answers into the computer and having them played back through the synthesizer.[1] Ruopp was using what is known as adaptive technology.

Adaptive technology includes a wide range of technologies—technologies which are increasingly computer based. Scanning systems allow an individual who is blind to take a printed text and have it read back to him or her aloud. Individuals who have cerebral palsy can use their head movements to guide an electronic beam across a special keyboard in order to communicate. A gifted student who is also learning disabled, and who has great difficulty reading, can use a talking word processor to write stories and improve her reading.[2] An adult with little or no control over his body movement, but who can still speak, can control his environment by talking into a computer that can recognize spoken commands.[3] An individual who can move only his eyes can type messages on a computer using his eye movements.[4]

In each of the cases described above, an individual has overcome a disability through the use of computer-based adaptive technology. This emerging and innovative technology has become possible because of the widespread proliferation and use of inexpensive computers.

In an earlier work, *Beyond the Gutenberg Galaxy*, one of the authors argues that the introduction of inexpensive personal computers in the late 1970s set in motion an intellectual, technological, and social revolution that parallels to a remarkable degree the invention of moveable type in Europe in the late sixteenth century.[5] Just as printing brought about the creation of a typographic culture, the advent of the microcomputer represents:

> a critical force that is bringing to an end typographic culture and creating in its place a post-typographic culture and consciousness. After 500 years Western society is leaving the Gutenberg Galaxy and entering a new universe. The microcomputer is the key to this universe.[6]

By drawing on the power of the computer, adaptive technology—as we will demonstrate throughout this work—is also part of this new universe.

THE COMPUTER AS A PROSTHETIC DEVICE IN THE COGNITIVE AND PHYSICAL DOMAINS

The idea of the computer as enhancing and extending the capabilities of individuals in the cognitive and physical domains is a relatively new concept for most people. Despite this fact, the literature in computer science includes discussions of this issue dating back to the early 1960s.

In 1963 Douglas C. Engelbart argued in his essay "A Conceptual Framework for the Augmentation of Man's Intellect,"[7] that it would be possible to augment human intelligence through the use of computers. As he explained:

By "augmenting man's intellect" we mean increasing the capability of a man to approach a complex
problem situation, gain comprehension to suit his
particular needs, and to derive solutions to problems. Increased capability in this respect is taken to
mean a mixture of the following: that comprehension can be gained more quickly; that better comprehension can be gained more quickly; that better
comprehension can be gained; that a useful degree
of comprehension can be gained where previously
the situation was too complex; that solutions can
be produced more quickly; that better solutions can
be produced; that solutions can be found where
previously the human could find none.[8]

Engelbart was talking about the use of computers with normal
populations, but his ideas apply equally well to individuals
who are cognitively limited or disabled. A child who is dyslexic
and has great difficulty reading can have a block of text on a
computer screen read aloud to her using adaptive technology.
A child who has difficulty learning mathematics can be assisted
in solving problems through the presentation of visual representations on the computer.

Engelbart argued that the effect which an individual has
on the world is essentially dependent on "what he can communicate to the world through his limited motor channels."[9] The
individual's communication, in turn, depends on what information he or she has received through his or her limited sensory
channels, his or her personal needs, and how he or she processes that information.[10] Using the computer and adaptive technology, an adult with a disorder like cerebral palsy, who has been
severely limited in her ability to communicate, can for the first
time convey her thoughts and feelings. While Engelbart refers
in his work to the augmentation of human intellect through the
use of the computer, we would make the distinction that in the
context of the individual with disabilities the computer and
adaptive technology have the potential not just to augment the
individual's intellect, but also to provide the means to reveal it.

The computer and adaptive technology provide the
means for the disabled individual to go beyond the ability to
communicate, to allow him or her to actually manipulate and

control the environment. Through the use of switches—on/off computer input devices—a physically disabled individual can control a thermostat, answer a phone, direct a robot device to bring food, or activate the motor on an electrically powered wheelchair. Using such applications in adaptive technology, the disabled individual can achieve personal independence by manipulating objects and symbols connected to mechanical devices.

CYBERSPACE, CYBERNETICS, AND CONTROL

Adaptive technology employs several different methods and techniques. Some of these methods and techniques involve the manipulation and control of physical devices, while others involve the manipulation and control of *cyberspace*—a term used by science fiction writers such as William Gibson to describe the "inner space" of the computer.[11] In his novels, and in the stories of authors like Vernor Vinge, individuals using simulations enter into computer-created realities. These realities may or may not be based on the real world. Thus a user may enter into a fantasy world like the one found in J. R. R. Tolkien's novel *The Lord of the Rings* in which sorcerers and magicians have real powers, in which elves and dwarfs can be turned into stone, and in which dragons can fly. In Vinge's novella *True Names*, an elderly woman living in a high-rise apartment in Connecticut uses her computer to assume the role of a powerful sorceress at war with other people in cyberspace.

Cyberspace can also create realties that closely replicate the real world. A flight simulator, for example, can provide a pilot with an experience of flying in a storm with a damaged engine, or any of a wide range of conditions that closely imitate real flying conditions.

The term cyberspace is based on Norbert Wiener's term *cybernetics*. Wiener derived cybernetics from the Greek word *kubernetes* or "steersman." In defining cybernetics, Wiener "classed communication and control together." In doing so, he explains that:

When I communicate with another person, I impart a message to him, and when he communicates back with me he returns a related message which contains information primarily accessible to him and not to me. When I control the actions of another person, I communicate a message to him, and although this message is in the imperative mood, the technique of communication does not differ from that of a message of fact. Furthermore, if my control is to be effective I must take cognizance of any messages from him which may indicate that the order is understood and has been obeyed.[12]

The use of adaptive technology, by definition, implies both communication and control. When an individual enters a simulation, he or she, is entering not only into a mode of communication, but also into a system of control.

In a simulation, control can be exercised by an individual manipulating a computer within cyberspace, or over an individual. This later case—that of control being exercised over an individual—involves the computer and its programs directing the individual. The question of to what extent the individual controls or is controlled by the computer is a fundamental ethical and moral issue that must be addressed by those interested in the use of adaptive technology and computers.

ON THE NON-NEUTRALITY OF THE COMPUTER

It is widely assumed that computers are a neutral technology; yet neither computers, nor the simulations that they create, are neutral. As Ted Nelson has argued, every simulation has a point of view.[13] C. A. Bowers addresses the same question from a slightly different perspective when he questions

...whether the technology is neutral; that is, neutral in terms of accurately representing, at the level of the software program, the domains of the real world in which people live.[14]

Bowers argues that computers must be understood as "part of the much more complex symbolic world that makes up our culture."[15] We must look at them in more than just a procedural context to better understand how they mediate and change our systems of knowledge and ways of interpreting the world around us.[16]

In this context—and more specifically the context of adaptive technology—we must ask what it is that the computer and its software selects for amplification and for reduction.[17]

In the case of a communication board used by individuals unable to produce speech, users are limited by the constraints of the board's program and hardware. If the device can only output messages that have been pre-programmed, then individuals attempting to communicate using the device may find themselves highly constrained. They may want to communicate a desire for a banana or another piece of fruit, while the device only indicates food. They may want to indicate concern, while the machine is only programmed to express anger. Limitations in hardware may mean that a device is incapable of being easily reprogrammed and must be sent to the manufacturer or a lab to be adapted to the specific needs of an individual.

In a software simulation, a physically disabled child may have the opportunity to sense some of the excitement that a fully enabled individual has when playing a game such as football or driving a race car. It should be emphasized, however, that the simulation that is created may have certain aspects of the experience amplified or reduced by what is or is not included in the program. For example, in a race car driving program is the race viewed from the perspective of the driver inside the car or from an overhead view that shows the race cars moving through the track in relationship to one another? In a simulated football game, does the quarterback get feedback from the crowd in the form of boos or cheers?—do weather conditions change and affect the condition of the field? and so on.

In the context of the examples cited, we are not arguing against the use of simulation, but instead are asking not only developers, but also users and enablers, to consider more carefully what it is that a program either emphasizes or de-emphasizes. In doing so, there should be an implicit recognition of the limitations inherent in a simulated environment. This question is particularly relevant with the emergence of new technologies such as virtual reality.

VIRTUAL REALITY AND ADAPTIVE
TECHNOLOGY

In the last few years a revolutionary simulation technology has begun to emerge, which has important implications for the field of adaptive technology. While still in its earliest stages of development, this technology, known as virtual reality, promises to rapidly develop in the near future and change in revolutionary ways how we approach and use computers.[18]

Many types of virtual reality systems have been developed. On one level, it could be argued that a sophisticated flight simulator represents a type of virtual reality system. More recently, however, virtual reality equipment has involved the use of sophisticated programs with devices such as eye-phones (a tiny pair of video screens that are mounted in front of each eye that provide stereo vision of a computer-created reality), data gloves (in which sensors lining one's hand communicate movement to a graphics computer), and stereo earphones and positional sensing equipment, through which one can enter a simulated computer environment.[19]

Autodesk's Cyberspace program, for example, lets architects and designers stroll through three-dimensional models by putting on stereoscopic goggles. A 3-D model surrounds the user and changes the perspective and point of view as the user turns or tilts his or her head, or walks forward, backwards or sideways. The user also wears a data glove wired with fiber optic sensors. Using the data glove, objects can be manipulated within the simulation that is created by the system. Doors can be opened and shut, objects grasped and a sense of function in "real space" gained in ways that have never been thought possible before.[20]

A preview of the possibilities with virtual reality can be seen in the holodeck device that is included in many of the episodes of the science fiction television program "Star Trek: The Next Generation." Users entering the holodeck are able to participate in virtual simulations that appear completely life-like. Characters on the program, while moving in their space-ship across the galaxy at enormous speeds, are able to visit a picnic spot and fishing hole on earth, or to assume the role of a historical character in the eighteenth century.

We are convinced that simulations of this type are the logical endpoint in the development of virtual reality systems. How long it will take before it is possible to experience the types of simulations that are available to the members of the crew of the *Enterprise* is of course impossible to precisely pre-dict. However, it seems reasonable that if computers and simu-lation programs continue to evolve as rapidly as they have in the past decade, Star Trek's holodeck—or something like it—will be part of our future fairly soon.

The implication of technologies such as virtual reality for individuals with disabilities is enormous. Imagine, for exam-ple, two individuals whose control over their bodies is limited to eye tracking movement. Connected to virtual reality sys-tems, they have the potential to move through cyberspace in a simulation that could allow them the illusion that they are fully mobile. In its most advanced application, this might involve implanting hardware in the various sectors of the brain that provide feeling and sensation. It is conceivable that indi-viduals who are almost totally paralyzed in the physical world could engage in touching and feeling and even sexual relations in a cyberspace world created with virtual reality techniques.

Of course serious questions arise. What is reality? Where does being a human and being a machine sort itself out? Do we lose something of our humanity by engaging in such tech-niques? These are serious questions that will have to be addressed in the future, as we advance into progressively more sophisticated applications and use of virtual reality.

ON THE HUMAN USE OF
HUMAN BEINGS

Returning to possible futures suggested by science fiction, on "Star Trek: The Next Generation," Jordie, the chief engineering officer for the *Enterprise*, is blind. A sensing device, which he wears like eyeglasses and which is connected directly to his brain, enables him to see. Such devices are in the early stages of development and, while today are only fully realized in science fiction, have the very real likelihood of coming into being in the near future. If such a scenario seems farfetched, consider the fact that cochlear implants have been used for several years now to transmit sounds via the neural pathways of deaf individuals.

Just how far such technologies might take us is suggested by Hans Moravec, a robotics researcher at Carnegie Mellon University. Moravec predicts, for example, that in the next generation we will have the potential to download a human intelligence onto a computer, where it will be able to direct and control robotic mechanisms.[21] The potential uses of such technology in a field such as adaptive technology are mindboggling.

Using technology of the type outlined by Moravec, it would be theoretically possible to have the consciousness of a paralyzed individual transferred to a robot, which could allow the individual to function in a day-to-day world. Will such possibilities be liberating or tragically dehumanizing? Would it be morally right to send a human consciousness in a robotic device into the deep reaches of space? What distinctions will be made between being human or being a machine?

Like Prospero in Shakespeare's *Tempest*, we and others interested in adaptive technology are faced with a "brave new world." It is a world fraught with perils and possibilities, which we must carefully consider and reflect upon as we enter into this remarkable new field.

2

COMPUTERS AND SPECIAL NEEDS

Approximately 43 million Americans, or one in six people, have some type of disability. Each year an additional 750,000 Americans become disabled, mainly through accidents. About two-thirds of the disabled population is of working age, and about two-thirds of this group is unemployed.[1] We assume throughout this work that computer-based adaptive technology can help these individuals more fully realize their potential. In this context, we are drawn to ideas articulated by Thomas Jefferson nearly two hundred years ago.

In his *Rockfish Gap Report* (1818) on the educational program at the University of Virginia, Jefferson outlined the aims of education in a democracy. According to Jefferson, education should provide a citizen with the means to transact his own business; to calculate for himself and preserve his ideas, contracts, and accounts in writing; to improve his morals and faculties through the ability to read; to help him fulfill his obligations and duties as a neighbor and as a more general member of the society; to provide him an understanding of his rights; and finally to give him the means by which to understand and engage in social relations.[2]

In essence, Jefferson was concerned with each individual becoming all that he or she was capable of being. We believe that adaptive technology can significantly contribute to this process for individuals with disabilities. Computers and adaptive technology can provide the means by which the disabled can gain access to the opportunities and insights provided by education and in turn the means by which to lead more productive and satisfying lives.

The following chapter provides an introduction to the four general areas of disability that can be addressed through the use of adaptive technology: (1) visual impairment, (2) hearing and speech impairment, (3) physical impairment, and (4) cognitive impairment. We also address the question of adaptive technology and equity, and introduce the fundamental elements that make up this new and exciting technology.

VISUAL IMPAIRMENT

The category of visually impaired includes both low vision and blind individuals. Visual impairment, even with correction, adversely affects an individual's educational performance.

Figure 2.1. The Navigator 80 from TeleSensory allows an individual to read one complete screen line at a time by translating the images on the screen into braille. Photo courtesy of TeleSensory.

Technology can be adapted for visually impaired individuals in a number of different ways. Input devices can include braille keyboards, scanning devices and voice input systems. Output devices include enlarged video, speech output, large ink print, braille print, and tactual output devices (Figure 2.1).

HEARING AND SPEECH IMPAIRMENT

Hearing loss can range from mild to profound or deaf, which in the case of the latter is so severe that the individual is unable to process linguistic information through hearing, even with amplification. The development of communication skills—speech in particular—can be affected by this condition. Speech impairment includes problems such as difficulty with articulation or voice, stuttering, or language disorders. For individuals who have hearing and speech impairments, computer-based speech output devices can demonstrate how to correctly pronounce and articulate words. Deaf individuals can speak words using voice input and see the representation of their speech on a computer display (Figure 2.2).

PHYSICAL IMPAIRMENT

Also referred to as motor impairment, physical impairment includes disabilities caused by congenital anomalies (such as missing limbs), by disease (such as poliomyelitis), and by other factors (such as cerebral palsy, amputations, fractures, or burns). Specific characteristics vary according to the nature and severity of the condition. Adaptive technology for individuals who have physical impairments comprises input devices such as keyboards with expanded target areas, handheld devices, voice input, switch input and eye controlled systems (Figure 2.3).

Figure 2.2. TeleBraille II (hearing) enables a deaf-blind person and another person using a TDD to have telephone communication. Photo courtesy of TeleSensory.

COGNITIVE IMPAIRMENT

Cognitively impaired includes individuals who are mentally retarded or who have one or more learning disabilities. Mental retardation is defined as significantly subaverage intellectual performance along with deficits in adaptive behavior. A learning disability is a disorder in one or more of the processes involved in understanding or in using language. This includes spoken or written language, which may affect an individual's ability to listen, think, speak, read, write, spell, or do mathematical calculations. Children with these types of disabilities may find it difficult to concentrate, have poor coordination, have difficulty with auditory or visual processing, have poor

Figure 2.3. The Headmaster from Prentke Romich is a computer access device that allows an individual who is unable to use his hands to operate a computer using head movement and activating a puff switch. Photo courtesy of Prentke Romich.

memory, and have difficulty in abstract reasoning and in making generalizations. Individuals with these disabilities can benefit from many of the same adaptive input and output devices used by individuals who are visually, hearing, speech, or motor impaired. A person who has coordination problems, for example, might benefit from an expanded keyboard. Someone with severe reading problems can often benefit from voice output systems (Figure 2.4).

Many of the problems associated with cognitive impairment are addressed by specialized software. A child with figure-ground discrimination problems, for example, can benefit significantly from programs that present only one item at a time, or which can be repeated as many times as needed by the learner.

Figure 2.4. Co:Writer is a word prediction program for reducing keystrokes and increasing the quantity and quality of written work for cognitively disabled individuals. Photo courtesy of Don Johnston, Incorporated.

COMPUTER HARDWARE

Problems associated with vision, hearing and speech, and physical and cognitive impairments can be addressed by different aspects of adaptive technology, all of which involve the computer and its peripheral devices. These aspects must be understood if the full potential and possibilities of adaptive systems are to be realized.

A computer is "any machine which can accept *data* in a prescribed form, process the data and supply the results of the processing in a specified format as information or as signals to control automatically some further machine or process."[3]

A computer accepts data through some type of input device (usually a keyboard). It processes data in a central processing unit and it presents the results through an output device (most commonly a video display terminal or monitor).

Adapting input and output devices is the key to using computers to enable individuals with disabilities. Much of the discussion in this book deals with different input and output devices that make the power of computing available to individuals with disabilities.

Computers require the use of large amounts of information stored as programs or as data files. Storage devices come in many different forms; the most widely used storage system is a disk drive, which transfers electronic information to the magnetic surface of a disk. Magnetic disks, although increasingly efficient, are limited by their storage capacity. Disks that were commonly in use during the late 1970s were available in 5$\frac{1}{4}$ inch format and had 143 kilobytes of storage. A byte is the amount of space needed to store approximately one character (a letter, number, punctuation mark, space, etc.) A kilobyte is 1,024 bytes, or the space needed to store approximately one thousand characters. A disk with 143 Kilobytes of storage capacity can store approximately 143,000 characters. Three and one-half inch disks can store 800 kilobytes. High-density magnetic disks currently in use can hold 1.44 megabytes of data (a megabyte equals approximately one million bytes). These disks can therefore store about 1.44 million characters.

Hard disks have capacities typically ranging from 100 to 560 megabytes. Hard disks use magnetic coated, rigid metal or glass recording surfaces to store data. Like the floppy disk, a hard disk is a random access storage device, which means that information can be accessed quickly regardless of where it is located on the disk. It has the advantage, however, of being able to store greater quantities of data than floppy disks.

The most advanced storage system currently in widespread use is optical memory, which uses laser technology. Optical discs often store thousands of times more information than magnetic disks. These discs are a high-density, random access medium that theoretically will not wear out, since nothing but a beam of light touches the disc. Data is encoded on the surface of a highly polished aluminum disc. This data is read by a low-power laser. At this time, videodiscs and CD-

ROM are the most widely used laser-based storage media, although other types such as DVI (Digital Video Interactive) and CD-I (Compact Disc-Interactive), WORM (write once read many), and erasable optical drives are becoming more popular.

One type of optical disc, the videodisc, typically measures twelve inches in diameter and can hold, depending on its format, either thirty or sixty minutes of television or film per side. It creates the image of motion by projecting still images in rapid succession and can have up to four discreet audio tracks, which can be used for music or voice. With a good videodisc player, any frame can be accessed in a few seconds. Programming is encoded on these discs as millions of tiny nonreflective pits on a reflective surface. Like CD-ROM technology, a beam of low-powered laser light hits either the pits or the reflective areas between pits, producing a high frequency signal that the player converts to television and stereo.[4] Video discs can incorporate as well as coordinate virtually all types of media, including films, transparencies, and books. Video discs can also incorporate Line 21 or closed captioning systems. Captions can be put onto a disc, which can then be seen using a special decoding system. Using a closed captioning system makes it possible for an individual who is hearing impaired to follow the story line and dialogue of a play, movie, or some other form of spoken performance.[5]

Another type of optical disc is the compact disc read-only memory (CD-ROM). This 4.7 inch optical disc contains digital information which can be used by the computer. A total of approximately two billion pits measuring three miles in length can be etched onto the surface of the aluminum that provides the recording medium for CD-ROM. This represents 640 megabytes of data, which is about 6 billion characters or the equivalent of 250,000 pages of typewritten information.[6] These discs can hold a huge amount of text, but only about seven minutes of video. To overcome this limitation, other formats such as CD-I and DVI can be used.

Compact Disc-Interactive format specifies how audio, video, graphics, text, and machine-executable code should be placed on a CD-ROM to provide full-motion, full screen capability. CD-I technology is still evolving.

Digital Video Interactive is another technology based on video compression and decompression. Video is digitized and compressed and transferred to a CD-ROM. During playback, DVI video is decompressed and displayed. Both CD-I and DVI provide large amounts of audio, graphics, full-motion video and computer programming to be placed on a CD-ROM.[7]

The tremendous storage capacity of CD-ROM, along with CD-I and DVI, provides great possibilities for enabling individuals with physical and cognitive limitations. The ability to store and access large amounts of data and to access full-motion video through the computer will enhance these technologies. For example, being able to provide prerecorded speech, which requires a great deal of storage space, rather than having to use digitized speech, is a significant advantage.

COMPUTERS AND ROBOTICS

Robots and robotic systems have a variety of potential applications and uses in the field of adaptive technology. The term robot comes from a 1920 play *R.U.R.* by the Czech playwright Karl Capek. The word robot literally means in Czech "forced labor" or "servitude." The dictionary defines robot as "any machine or mechanical device that operates automatically with human-like skill."

Robots have mainly been developed and used in industrial applications. Industrial robots include those that do such diverse tasks as painting, welding, and assembling. Robots in this category often perform jobs that are highly repetitious or dangerous. Besides their industrial use, robotic systems are frequently included in toy devices. Toy robots, although limited in complexity, can be used to demonstrate robotic concepts. They incorporate many of the elements of more powerful industrial robots. Limited educational uses of robots include devices such as the LOGO Turtle, which is a simple motorized device attached to a desktop computer by an umbilical cord, and which responds to commands from a keyboard.[8]

Robotic devices have a wide range of potential applications for individuals with disabilities. As computers become less and less expensive, as well as easier to program and use, we will see more and more uses for them in the field of adaptive technology. Using a computer controlled by an appropriate adaptive input device, an individual can direct a robot to do the tasks that he or she is incapable of doing. A robotic arm can be activated by a disabled individual to pull a book from a shelf, turn a page, or turn on a light. The technology is available to create robots that can take the place of attendants for individuals with disabilities. These robots can lift a person from a chair to a bed, get the newspaper, prepare a meal, and even act as a security or fire alarm. Sophisticated servo control mechanisms on a prosthetic arm make it possible for an amputee to grasp and lift objects.

As discussed in chapter 1, robotic experts such as Hans Moravec predict that in the next twenty or thirty years we will be able to actually download a human consciousness onto a computer. If this does in fact occur, it is a reasonable assumption that we would want to give that consciousness mobility in the physical world. This would be achieved through robotic devices. Although it borders on the realm of science fiction, it may be reasonable in the future for individuals with disabilities to talk about replacing their imperfect human bodies with robotic bodies.[9] Is this acceptable? Why is it acceptable to have a robotic limb, but not a totally robotic body? Where is the dividing line? Obvious ethical issues come to mind. But, is it any different for an individual to use a non-robotic prosthetic arm or a motorized arm, or for that matter false teeth or eyeglasses, as compared to a completely robotic body?

TYPE I AND TYPE II USES
OF COMPUTERS

A variety of metaphors and models have been used to describe computers. Taylor talks about the computer in the context of its use in the schools as a tool, tutor, or tutee.[10] Seymour Papert describes computers as metaphysical machines.[11] Many educators concerned with the adaption and use of computers in the schools during the 1980s saw them as machines that would usher in a new micro-millennium. Zealots argued that by simply exposing students to computers tremendous benefits would be derived.

Cleborne D. Maddux in his article "Issues and Concerns in Special Education Microcomputing," argues that special educators have reached a crossroad in the educational use of computers. According to Maddux, two types of computer applications exist: Type I and Type II. Type I applications involve using the computer to perform, more easily or quickly, tasks that special educators have always done. Type II applications make new and better procedures available to special educators. Almost any sort of adaptive technology represents a Type II application; of course, how effective an application is another question.[12]

Maddux argues that, while Type I applications are extremely important, in and of themselves they are insufficient to significantly change education. By themselves, Type I applications of computers do not justify their expense to the schools. The use of computers in not only special education, but education in general, can only be justified if Type II applications in which new and better ways of teaching are employed. Maddux argues that if educational microcomputing turns out to be a be a failure, like previous technologies that have been introduced into the classroom, it will be because the majority of educational applications and uses have not gone beyond Type I.[13]

Focusing on Type I uses of computers has led educators to address questions of how to use computers rather than why use them. Edward Cain argues that in doing so, special educators have neglected the need to develop a "philosophical rationale for the use of computers with handicapped children and adults."[14] According to Cain, in order to answer the question "Why use computer technology with exceptional children?" one must first ask "What is the ultimate goal of special education?" If, as we have argued earlier in this chapter, the goal of special education is to assist individuals with disabilities in reaching their maximum potential, then the use of computers and adaptive technology—particularly in Type II applications—is critically important. This leads to the question of adaptive technology and equity.

ADAPTIVE TECHNOLOGY AND EQUITY

Adaptive technology cannot only provide individuals with the means by which to improve the quality of their day-to-day lives, but can also provide them with the opportunity to compete on an equal footing in our culture. Whether or not an individual with disabilities has access to this technology can involve important issues of fairness and equity.

A gifted student who is blind can function in a normal academic setting if given access to a computer with a braille keyboard and a voice output system. An individual who is hearing impaired can learn to speak more clearly with the assistance of a voice recognition and training system. An individual with severe physical impairments can complete written work if provided with a computer with switch input devices and scanning software. Individuals with learning impairments can remediate areas that they are deficient in while taking advantage of their natural strengths and abilities.

If individuals with disabilities are empowered through new adaptive technologies, then those disabled individuals who do not have access to these technologies face even greater problems in terms of equity. By enabling only a limited portion of the population through adaptive technology, those without access to it fall not only behind normal populations, but also behind those disabled individuals who have access to the new systems.

Sigmund Freud in his book *Civilization and Its Discontents* argued that man has become a kind of prosthetic god. Commenting on Freud's insight, Witold Rybczynski argues that:

> Not being able to run very fast or for very long he has grafted onto himself additional feet, until he can travel farther and faster than any other animal, and not only on land but also on and under water and in the air. He can reinforce his eyes with glasses, telescopes, and microscopes. Thanks to orbiting satellites he can, without displacing himself, count wildebeest in the African veld, or missile silos outside Novosibirsk. Lacking the dolphin's ability to communicate great distances, he amplifies his voice with the aid of radio waves. In addition to his genetic code, which he shares with all other living things, he has acquired a perpetually growing communal memory in the shape of the written word, the photograph and the recording.[15]

If man is indeed the "prosthetic god," then the use of adaptive technology is a logical extension of what we are as human beings. When we provide adaptive technology for disabled individuals, we are simply providing them with tools to communicate and extend their range of activity. In this sense, what is being done is no different than providing a person with a car to go to the store, or a telephone to talk to a friend across the country.

Yet these extensions of ourselves are not without costs— both moral and financial. While we may see adaptive technology as expanding opportunities for individuals and creating greater equity, we must be very conscious of the price that we pay. What do we lose and what do we gain through using the technology? As we engage ourselves increasingly with the new technology, we must constantly ask what the costs are at all levels, and whether we are truly providing what is best and most needed by the individual.

These are not easy questions to answer. In the following pages, we will continue to address these questions and others involving specific adaptations and uses of the technology.

3

INPUT AND OUTPUT DEVICES

Underlying the general field of adaptive technology and special education is the larger issue of interface design. Computers from an interface perspective work on two different levels: (1) they display information and execute commands (output), and (2) they have commands sent to them (input) so that a function can be executed.

Interface issues face us constantly in a technological world. A steering wheel is a machine/human interface that allows us to steer a car or truck. A fork is an interface system that makes it easier to transfer food from a plate to one's mouth. Many different types of interfaces can be used, and these have typically evolved and become more sophisticated over the passage of time. For example, sometime during the early Renaissance period forks were introduced as interface devices for eating in Western culture. Prior to that time spoons were widely used to assist in eating, and before that bare hands.

Whether or not a fork is an ideal interface device for eating is open to debate. In many parts of Asia, the same needs are fulfilled by using chopsticks. Are chopsticks better interface devices for eating than forks? This question is not necessarily an easy one to answer. Why one interface device is used over another may often be rooted as much in tradition and culture as in actual need.

What about mixing interface devices (i.e. using forks, spoons and knives) to eat? When we use a full table setting at a formal dinner, we assign specialized interface devices to different courses of the meal. We use the salad fork to eat salad, a soup spoon to eat soup, a regular fork for the main course, and so on. In the computer world, mixed interface systems include the use of a keyboard with a mouse (input) or a video display terminal with sound from a speaker (output).

This chapter outlines the basic principles underlying input and output devices for computers and individuals with special needs. In this context, it needs to be understood that standard interface devices are insufficient to meet the needs of the individual with special needs. What adaptive technology does is provide alternative pathways for the individual to interact (input) and produce actions by means of a computer (output).

Michael Chen and Frank Leahy in their essay "A Design for Supporting New Input Devices" describe four "point-counterpoints" involving the use of computer interfaces. These include: (1) alternative ways of performing the same task, (2) shortcuts that make a task easier to perform, (3) additional tools that make a task easier to perform, and (4) multiple devices working together to make a task possible or easier to perform.[1] These four point-counterpoints represent the key factors in developing enabling technology that uses computers. Although not referred to directly, they underlie most of our discussion of input and output devices in this chapter.

A standard computer uses a keyboard for input and a monitor for the output. Typically, computers are modified in an adaptive or assistive context to address hearing and speech, vision, motor and learning impairments. The computer can be modified by adaptations to existing technologies or through assistive technologies, which are devices created specifically for individuals with disabilities.

INPUT DEVICES

The standard keyboard is the most common computer input device. Individuals with various types of disabilities often find it difficult or even impossible to communicate with the computer through a standard keyboard. A number of alternative means, however, are available by which they can access the computer. Finding an appropriate input device is the most important factor in providing individuals with disabilities access to computers and related technology.

Standard Keyboards

A standard keyboard can be modified in one or more of the following ways. (1) Keys can be color coded, or have decals with symbols fastened to them to help users locate certain keys more easily (Figures 3.1 and 3.2). (2) A template or overlay can be set over a keyboard so that only certain keys show. When using a piece of software that requires only a few keys, a coded key or a template can make using the computer much easier. (3) A keyguard can be placed over a standard keyboard to allow only one key to be hit at a time (Figure 3.3). A keyguard is made of firm plastic and fits over all the keys on the keyboard. Holes large enough for a finger or a pointer to fit through and

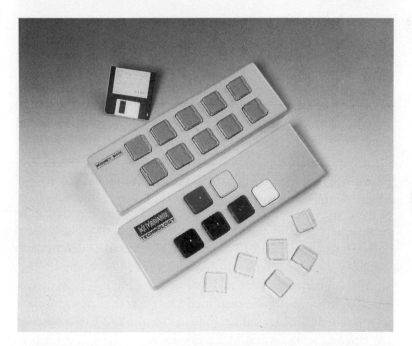

Figure 3.1. Matchbox Keyboard Covers from Don Johnston Developmental Equipment are snapped over designated keys on a regular keyboard to help users find selected keys more easily. Photo courtesy of Don Johnston, Incorporated.

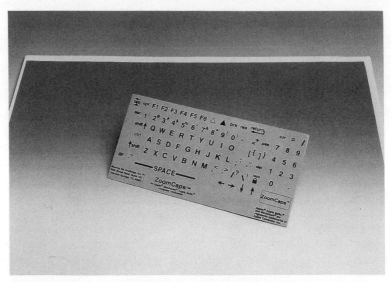

Figure 3.2. ZoomCaps key labels from Don Johnston Developmental Equipment can be stuck on selected keys on a standard computer keyboard to increase visibility for the user. Photo courtesy of Don Johnston, Incorporated.

press one key at a time are placed above each key. Even if an individual has to rest his or her hand or palm on the keyboard for stability, a keyguard makes it easier to press only one key at a time. Since keyboards are different for different computers, keyguards in most instances must be custom-made for specific keyboards. (4) The repeat function on a keyboard can be slowed down or disabled so that users who are unable to release keys quickly enough will not accidentally repeat characters or commands. (5) Programs can be used which make it possible for individuals who cannot press two or more keys simultaneously to be able to do so by pressing two keys in succession. (6) Keys can be redefined on the keyboard so they are in alphabetical order rather than using the QWERTY system. (7) Specialized command functions or macros can be programmed into particular keys. (8) For visually impaired individuals, braille or raised characters set on the surface of keys can make keyboard functions accessible.

Figure 3.3. The Keyguard from Don Johnston Developmental Equipment stabilizes and positions the hand of the user over the computer keyboard. Photo courtesy of Don Johnston, Incorporated.

Alternative Keyboards

Alternative keyboards differ significantly in their design from standard keyboards. The Muppet Learning Keys (Figure 3.4), for example, is a keyboard designed primarily for use by young children. The keys on the Muppet keyboard are not only larger, but have more space between them than do the keys on a standard keyboard. In addition, the keys on the Muppet keyboard are in alphabetical order and use pictures to designate certain functions.

The PowerPad is a touch sensitive keyboard which measures twelve by twelve inches (Figure 3.5). The PowerPad can be divided into as few as two or as many as 144 separate target areas. Each of these target areas can be programmed to generate voice and visual output. Supporting software provides the

Figure 3.4. Muppet Learning Keys provide a keyboard with upper and lower-case letters in alphabetical order with large target areas and action buttons. Courtesy of WINGS for Learning/Sunburst, Incorporated.

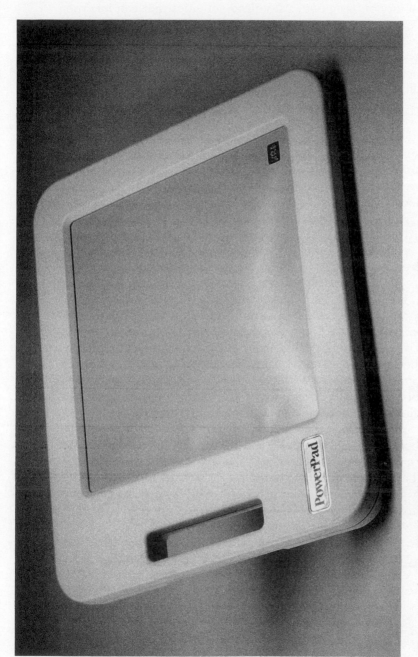

Figure 3.5. The PowerPad provides a large surface that can be divided into different sized target/input zones. Photo courtesy of Laureate Learning Systems, Incorporated.

capability of designing customized activities that can incorporate speech, text, and graphics.

The Keasyboard is a zero pressure alternative keyboard for the Apple II computer. Key selections are made by touching a key area outlined by a built-in keyguard. No pressure is required, since contact is detected by means of an optical electric sensing device.

Condensed keyboards or mini-keyboards are manufactured by a number of different companies. These keyboards make it possible for individuals with a very limited range of motion to reach all of the keys. An individual who cannot move his or her arm, but who can control the movement of his or her fingers would, for example, use this type of keyboard.

An example of a specialized version of a condensed keyboard is the BAT from Infogrip. It has seven keys, five of which are positioned directly under the fingers and thumb. Data is entered by pressing combinations of keys. It can be used with only one hand or with both hands and is available in braille.

Expanded keyboards, such as the Unicorn keyboard, use large touch sensitive boards over which templates can be laid. Expanded keyboards can be programmed to operate in several different ways. They can simply emulate a standard keyboard, or the touch sensitive areas can be defined by the user. Speech output devices can be added to this type of keyboard. Expanded keyboards like the Unicorn can be held on the lap or placed on the floor or the lapboard of a wheelchair.

The Comfort Keyboard is a three-sectioned adjustable keyboard for individuals who lack the strength or capability to use a conventional keyboard effectively. The sections for the left hand, right hand and the numeric keypad can be independently separated, raised, lowered, rotated, and tilted to an unlimited number of positions.

A touch sensitive screen such as the TouchWindow is an input device that enables a user to touch a video screen to make a selection (Figure 3.6). This input method is particularly effective because the focus of both input and output are on the screen; all the user has to do is point.

Another input option is provided by software which places an image of a keyboard on the computer screen, allowing individuals who cannot access the standard keyboard to perform all keyboard functions using a mouse, trackball, or

Figure 3.6. The TouchWindow attaches to the computer monitor and provides access to the computer by touching the screen. Photo courtesy of Laureate Learning Systems, Incorporated.

head pointer. This software is available for the Windows environment, as well as for Macintosh computers. It includes such helpful features as word prediction and a dictionary that can be easily modified to meet specific needs.

Hand-Held Devices

A mouse is a hand-held input device with which the user moves a cursor to any point on a screen and, by "clicking" a button on the mouse, activates an item on the screen of the computer. A rollerball or trackball is a stationary type of mouse.

The joystick is another type of hand-held input device that can be used to move a cursor on a screen. Buttons on a joystick can be used to activate a particular response depending on the position of the cursor. This is an inexpensive input device, and requires far less fine motor skill than a keyboard. Joysticks are widely used in computer games.

A final hand-held input device is the light pen. Light pens look like an ordinary pen and allow the user to interact directly with whatever appears on a computer monitor by shining the pen's light directly onto the monitor where it is recorded as an X-Y coordinate. Using a light pen, one can draw or execute commands.

Graphics Tablets

Graphics tablets are touch sensitive surfaces for electronic drawing. Some use a pen attached to the board and others use a stylus for pointing and drawing. What is drawn on the pad is displayed on the screen and can also be stored in memory and printed out on paper. The Koala Pad is one popular graphics tablet; it can be used by itself to produce graphics and also works with other graphics software.

Special Supplementary Computer Boards

Supplementary computer boards provide alternative access or input to the computer through such modes such as Morse code, single or multiple switch scanning or devices like mini- or expanded keyboards. Cards of this type are available for many types of computers including both MS-DOS machines, and computers included as part of the Apple II and Macintosh series.

The Adaptive Firmware Card, for example, is a card that can be put in the slot of any Apple II computer. It is a keyboard emulator that enables individuals with disabilities to use adaptive input devices with standard software, so that users are not limited to the software that has been written specifically for a particular device. For example, an individual can access any software through a switch. The software can be presented in scanning mode for switch access or one or more switches can be used to input Morse code, which the Adaptive Firmware Card translates into keyboard characters.

The Ke:nx (pronounced "connects") is the equivalent of the Adaptive Firmware Card for the Macintosh computer (Figure 3.7). With this interface, individuals can use alternate input devices to access Macintosh programs including videodiscs and CD-ROMs. Using Ke:nx's assisted keyboard mode, a standard keyboard can be adjusted for one-handed access, or the entire keyboard can be redefined with special functions. Simultaneous keystrokes can be executed by touching keys sequentially. The alternate keyboard mode provides for use of an expanded keyboard or a mini-keyboard. Scanning and Morse code input are also provided through the Ke:nx. An access mode for visually impaired individuals provides spoken output through the computer in which the board is resident. Ke:nx also makes it possible to change the size of the print on the computer screen to make it more readable for individuals with limited vision.

AccessDOS is a set of software programs that provides users with disabilities access to the IBM computer keyboard. It provides extended keyboard, mouse, and sound access for IBM DOS users and is free of charge to individuals with disabilities.

Switches

Switches are on/off devices that are activated by contact or by detection of motion, sound, or light. They can provide individuals with severe motor impairments the opportunity to independently operate devices such as battery powered toys, communication devices, environmental controls, or computers.

Figure 3.7. The Ke:nx is a transparent keyboard and mouse emulator that lets the user run standard software through a single switch, scanning, Morse code, alternate keyboards and ASCII format. Photo courtesy of Don Johnston, Incorporated.

There are many commercially made switches as well as countless variations of homemade or specially adapted mechanisms. Switches vary in a number of ways including the means used to activate them, their sensitivity, feedback, size, shape, and color. The features of a switch should be compatible with the individual's motor ability and adapted to whatever body part the individual can best use. Types of switches include (1) Push switches, which are activated with pressure. The sensitivity of these switches can vary from requiring only light pressure to others that are more resistant. This type of switch can make a clicking sound, which provides feedback to the user that contact has been made. Push switches can be activated by moving almost any part of the body (Figure 3.8). (2) Mercury switches, which are activated when a slight movement causes the mercury inside the switch to make contact with an electrical contact. Mercury switches provide no auditory feedback to the user. They must be attached to a movable body part such as the head or arm. (3) Pneumatic or puff and sip switches, which are activated by blowing or sucking air (Figure 3.9). These types of switches are frequently used by individuals who have no other controllable body movement. (4) Infrared switches, which are activated by moving something across an infrared beam. This can be done by blinking an eye, or by sweeping an arm or hand across the switch's beam. These types of switches can be used by individuals who have only limited motor control, as well as by individuals capable of much greater degrees of motion. (5) Light activated switches, which are activated by a beam of light. These typically are operated by an individual manipulating a light beam, which activates a switch. In its simplest form, a focused light is attached to a headband and then pointed by the individual turning his or her head (Figure 3.10). (6) Voice or sound activated switches which are turned on or off by a sound. Individuals with no controllable movement can use their voices or other sounds such as whistling or hissing.

Optical pointers provide input by using head, hand, mouth, shoulder, and other body motions. The sensor is a small camera that is plugged into a computer port and a small reflector worn by the user. Switches can be used as computer input devices through scanning or Morse code.

Scanning. Scanning (not to be confused with text or image scanning for the purposes of digitizing) is a method of choosing a desired picture or symbol. Items are presented one at a time and the individual must indicate which item he or she wishes to select.

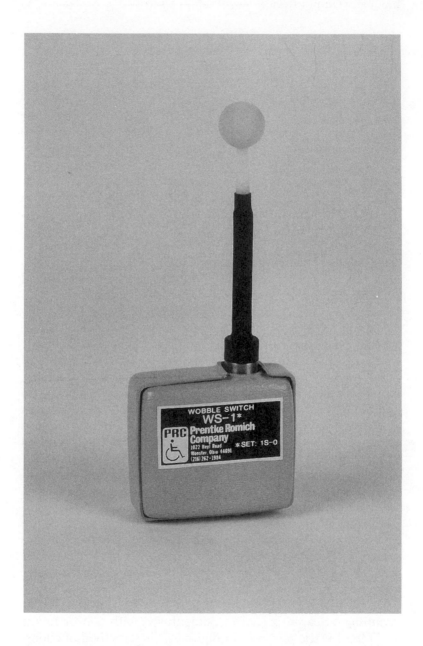

Figure 3.8. The Wobble Switch manufactured by Prentke Romich is a single switch that can be activated by gross movements. Photo courtesy of Prentke Romich.

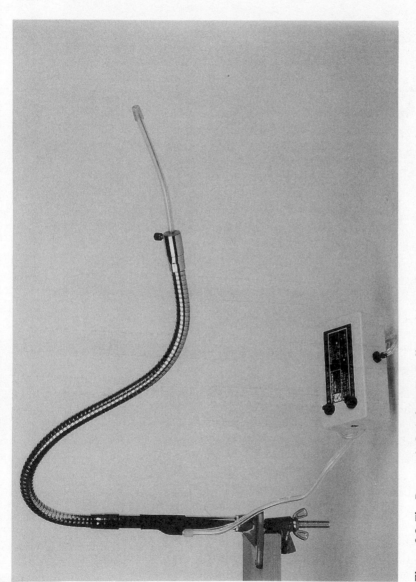

Figure 3.9. The Pneumatic Switch or Sip-Puff Switch manufactured by Prentke Romich is a breath-activated dual switch. Sipping activates one switch while puffing activates another. Photo courtesy of Prentke Romich.

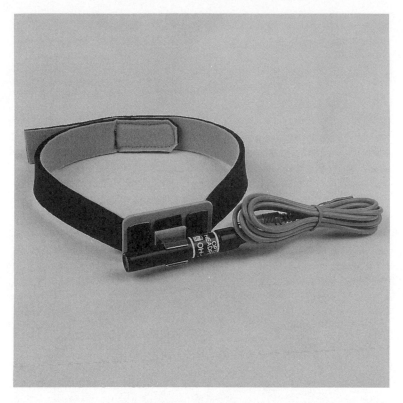

Figure 3.10. The Optical Headpointer manufactured by Prentke Romich allows the user to select items by pointing his or her head at a desired location such as computer screen. Photo courtesy of Prentke Romich.

Scanning can be manual or electronic. A simple example involving scanning would be a teacher saying a list of words or showing one picture at a time and having a child indicate with a nod or some other gesture when the desired word was said or the picture shown. Electronic scanning can be in the form of a clock scanner in which an arrow moves around a circle like the hand of a clock and an individual uses a switch to stop the pointer at a desired image.

Group item scanning involves first scanning by groups and then scanning each item individually. With word processing, for example, rather than scanning each letter of the alphabet, groups of letters are presented and the individual chooses the group with the desired letter and then chooses the letter from that group. Thus an individual writing a letter would begin the salutation by activating a switch to select the cluster of letters that contain "D" (ABCDE). From within that cluster the user would choose the letter "D" (ABCDE). By operating in this way, group item scanning eliminates the need for going through the entire alphabet to select a single letter.

Some scanning devices are equipped with speech output capabilities so that each symbol can be verbalized as it is presented. Scanning requires a minimal amount of physical control and can be done with a single switch, joystick, mouse, or by hitting a single key or area on an alternate keyboard. Speed can be adjusted to suit the ability of the individual. However, scanning is quite difficult because it requires an understanding of one to one correspondence, good visual skills, and good attention to task. Scanning should be used only by individuals for whom direct selection—i.e. looking at or pointing to a picture or symbol directly—is not possible.

Morse Code. Morse code can be entered using a switch to send a sequence of dots and dashes to form a character. Dots are represented by a short burst of electrical current and dashes by longer bursts. These short and longer bursts can be input using a single switch. An individual with the cognitive skills to learn Morse code and the physical ability to activate a switch can input information into the computer quite efficiently using Morse code.

A supplementary access device such as the Adaptive Firmware Card or the Ke:nx are required in order for the computer to accept Morse code input.

Vision-Controlled Input Devices

Eyescan is an eye position communication device consisting of a special pair of glasses to measure eye position and a computer to generate either written or spoken output. The individual looks at a computer terminal display of thirty cells that contain letters, words, or special functions. The computer senses when a particular cell has been chosen via a grid on the eyeglass lens and performs the appropriate function.

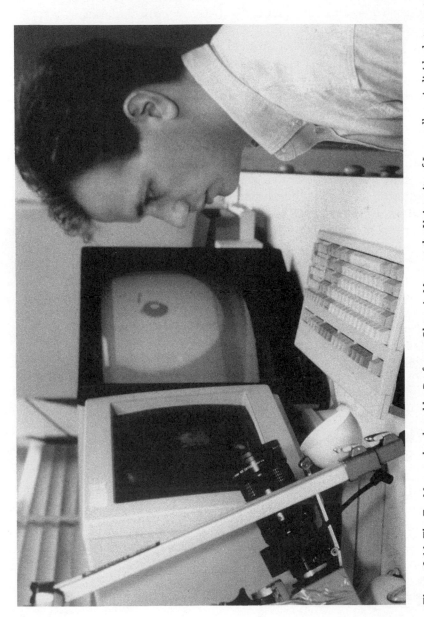

Figure 3.11. The EyeMouse, developed by Professor Glenn A. Myers at the University of Iowa, allows individuals to control a computer cursor through the movement of their eyes. Photo courtesy of Glenn A. Myers.

The EyeMouse[2] is another input device that lets individuals with disabilities control a computer through eye movements (Figure 3.11). The system includes a closed-circuit TV camera that tracks the pupil of the eye and an infrared light that illuminates the pupil. Eye movement is monitored by tracking the center of the pupil with a video camera. Changes in the position of where the individual is looking are converted into a standard mouse signal which is sent to the mouse port of a computer. Receiving the signal, special computer software responds accordingly.

The Eyegaze system is another direct-select vision-controlled system. Individuals with motor disabilities can perform a variety of functions including speech synthesis, environmental control, game playing, typing, using a telephone, and operating many types of software simply by looking at keys displayed on the monitor. The system is able to determine the direction of the eye's gaze using an infrared light reflecting off the cornea. To be able to use this system, individuals must have good control over at least one eye and over their head movement.

Voice-Activated Input Devices

Voice input technology allows an individual to speak words or phrases into a computer and have the computer recognize what has been said. Voice input can be used with almost any software. It has been limited, however, by the fact that devices using this technology have to be initialized for each user so pitch and accents unique to each individual can be recognized.

With voice input technology, the user's speech patterns are converted into digital data and stored, so that when the same words or patterns are repeated the computer can recognize them. A voice activated computer system by Kurzweil, called VOICE, does not require previous initialization of the computer for each new user's voice. It has a high degree of recognition for most users. This system gives individuals the ability to run word processing, spreadsheet, database, and other applications by speaking into a microphone. Macintosh computers also have the technology to automatically respond to each new user's voice.

Another example of a voice input system is the Dragon-Dictate System, which consists of hardware and software that turn an MS-DOS computer into a voice-driven typewriter. Words spoken into a microphone are typed out, with spacing and punctuation automatically provided. There are now several voice recognition systems which enable the computer to learn a thousand or more spoken commands. Many of these systems can also provide spoken responses to the user's commands.

Voice input technology is in the early stages of development, but its potential is highly promising. For individuals who cannot speak clearly but who can produce consistent sounds, the computer can learn to recognize these sounds as commands or as the words they represent. A speech synthesizer can then be used to produce clearly spoken words.

OUTPUT DEVICES

There are far fewer output devices than input devices available for computers. The main output devices include monitors, sound and printing devices. Essentially, adaptive technology modifies these three types of output devices to meet the special needs of different individuals. Since computers are primarily dependent on visual output as the basis for the user interface, adaptations are made most often for visually impaired individuals.

Monitors

Computer monitors are described in many different ways and involve a wide variety of technologies. Cathode ray tubes, video display units, and liquid crystal displays are terms that are used to describe different and sometimes the same "screen" or display technology. These devices, no matter what they are called, or what technology they are specifically based on, represent the main output device found on most computers.

The main adaptation of monitors is to enlarge the text and graphic representations presented on them. Video enlarging

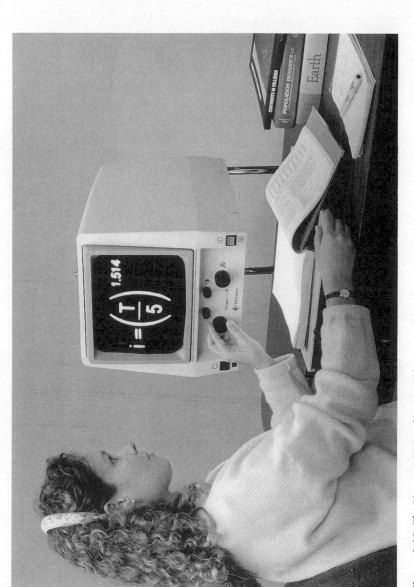

Figure 3.12. The Voyager CCD video magnifier manufactured by Telesensory enlarges images to forty-five times their original size. Photo courtesy of TeleSensory.

devices include closed circuit television (CCTV), large print display processors, and computer image enlarging systems (Figure 3.12). Closed circuit television provides a high level of clarity and flexibility and is easy to use. Any written material can be magnified up to 60 times by a CCTV. Magnification, brightness and contrast can be adjusted to fit individual needs. Large print display processors (LPDPs) enlarge each character displayed on a computer monitor to five or six inches in height. Computer image-enlarging systems also magnify computer monitor output, generally from two to twenty times. Certain types of software produce enlarged output without using any adaptive computer hardware.

An interesting adaptation of visual display systems for the visually impaired using tactile feedback is the Optacon (Optical-to-Tactile Converter). This device uses 144 electrically activated pins to translate printed material into raised, vibrating letters that are readable by touch (Figure 3.13). The raised print is not braille, but is a tactile counterpart of print symbols. A hand-held camera is passed over the print and the image is translated into the representation on the tactile display screen. Similar principles are used to produce braille output.

Printers

Printer output can be adapted in two ways: using large fonts, or using braille. Large print documents can be produced using word processing programs with large fonts. Most dot matrix, inkjet, thermal, and laser printers have the capability of supporting expanded print and type fonts. Braille printers print raised-dot characters, which can be read tactually (Figure 3.14). These types of printers have only recently become inexpensive enough for individuals and schools to easily afford them. They can be used not only by visually impaired students, but also by teachers to produce braille-printed materials for students.

Speech and Sound

The two most common ways to produce speech output are speech synthesis and speech digitization. Speech synthesis (often referred to as "text-to-speech") involves taking whatever

Figure 3.13. The Optacon print reading aid makes print accessible to blind people by translating print into a tactile array. Photo courtesy of TeleSensory.

Figure 3.14. The VersaPoint Braille printer from TeleSensory prints Braille characters and tactile graphics. Photo courtesy of TeleSensory.

is typed into a computer and converting it into synthetic speech. This technology produces voice output using the phonemes that constitute speech. Speech synthesis devices come with a set of rules that enable the computer to translate text into speech using these rules and rule exceptions. The greater the number of rule exceptions provided, the higher the quality of speech produced. This method can generate an unlimited vocabulary rather than limiting the user to prerecorded words. Synthesized speech does not require the use of a great deal of memory and is inexpensive. Synthesized speech devices, however, produce a somewhat mechanical and robot-like sound (Figure 3.15).

Digitized speech has the most human quality. It can capture intonations and accents. A human voice is recorded, digitized, compressed, and stored as data on a disk. When this data is played back, the identical sounds are heard, like a recording. However this method is limited in that it produces

Figure 3.15. The Echo II speech synthesizer is an internal speech card that comes with a speaker with volume control and a headphone jack. Photo courtesy of Laureate Learning Systems, Incorporated.

only words that have been previously recorded. Digitized speech uses a great deal of storage space, which is a problem with educational software that is produced on floppy magnetic disks. However, the use of optical discs, such as CD-ROM, with much greater memory capacity than magnetic disks, will facilitate the increased use of digitized speech.

Concern about the intelligibility of robot-like synthesized speech has generated research with adults and children. On the positive side, studies have shown that not only are adults with disabilities able to understand this speech but also children as young as three years of age can learn to understand the synthesized speech. However, children were better able to understand a more natural sounding voice. Even though individuals can understand synthesized speech, the greater intelligibility of digitized speech makes it worth the support of its further development.

CONCLUSION

Input and output devices will continue to evolve in the years to come. During the past decade we have seen the development of increasingly sophisticated devices. In the early 1980s, for example, most computer input was through keyboards. A decade later, we are seeing the increasingly widespread use of sensing devices such as infrared and sound activated switches, as well as sensors that can be activated though biofeedback provided by changes in blood pressure and brain wave patterns. Output devices have moved from very primitive loudspeakers and video terminals to wraparound virtual reality systems that include stereo vision goggles and extremely high quality stereo sound.

New developments involving interfaces and adaptive technology will be driven by improvements in graphic hardware and software systems. Essentially, as more powerful and sophisticated systems become available, we will be able to develop increasingly useful devices for the disabled.

It is clear that as we develop new and more innovative systems of adaptive technology, we also have an increasing need to update and retrain individuals. We need to develop increasingly effective ways of not only disseminating information about new technologies as they become available, but also of making their use simple enough so that they can be readily adapted and used.

It should be noted that more and more standard computer systems are able to accommodate adaptive input and output devices. An important challenge in the near future is to make sure that adaptive technology can be easily transferred across different hardware platforms, rather than be limited to just a few systems.

Interface design and the development of creative input and output systems, represents one of the most exciting areas of development in adaptive technology. As new generations of sophisticated computers and their software come on line, so too are new possibilities presented in terms of interface design. We have only just begun to explore what can be accomplished. We should be able to greatly expand the possibilities currently available to individuals with disabilities, and in doing so greatly increase the richness of their lives and experiences.

4

ADAPTIVE TECHNOLOGY AND THE PHYSICALLY AND VISUALLY IMPAIRED

In the previous chapters we have discussed how computers can be used to enhance and extend the cognitive and physical capabilities of individuals, as well as some of the techniques that can be used to adapt computers for specific individual needs. In this chapter, we look in more detail at the use of adaptive technology to assist individuals who have physical impairments, as well as those who are visually impaired.

PHYSICAL IMPAIRMENT

Physical impairment can involve the loss of physical movement, or a weakness or change in normal motor control. Some physical impairments are present at birth; others are acquired as a result of illness, accident, or unknown causes. Loss of movement is often caused by damage to the nervous system, particularly the spinal cord, or by physical trauma such as severe fractures, burns or the amputation of a limb.

A condition such as cerebral palsy, which is one of the most prevalent physical impairments in children, produces disturbances of voluntary motor control. Its manifestations range from clumsy and awkward movements to little or no coordinated movement. Other conditions such as muscular dystrophy, multiple sclerosis and amyotrophic lateral sclerosis, produce similar types of changes in physical functioning. Conditions that result in loss of motor control, such as cerebral palsy, often produce other problems as well. For example, individuals with cerebral palsy can have related speech problems, as well as impaired hearing or vision. They may also be cognitively impaired, but this is not always the case.[1]

As discussed in chapter 3, the keyboard is the standard computer input device. For individuals with physical impairments, using a standard keyboard may not only be difficult, but often impossible. Adaptations such as keyguards, expanded or mini-keyboards, touch screens, hand-held devices, such as a mouse or joystick, and switches enable physically impaired individuals to use the computer. Switches can be used for scanning programs or for Morse code input. Learning Morse code requires some time and effort, but it has been found to be considerably faster than scanning. Studies have shown that competent Morse code users can input text and alphanumeric data almost as rapidly as keyboard users.

Switches can also be used with a keyboard emulator such as Altkey. This program provides control of most MS-DOS based software with one or two switches. A Shareware program for MS-DOS computers called No-Keys provides keyboard-like input using a mouse or other hand-held device. No-Keys is intended for individuals who cannot physically use a keyboard, but can only make small motions with their hands and fingers. No-Keys displays a window containing text characters on the screen, to be used with a mouse cursor. When the mouse is clicked on a character, the computer responds as if that character had been typed on the keyboard. This software makes most keyboard-input programs accessible through a mouse.

Similar software called WordWriter is available for the Macintosh computer. In this software, letters and words are displayed in a moveable window on the screen and are selected with a mouse, trackball, or LipStick. The LipStick is an alternative input device to the Macintosh mouse and is compatible with all Macintosh applications. It can be operated with the lips, chin, cheek, or other parts of the body which have minimal movement.

The Half-QWERTY keyboard is an example of an adaptation of the keyboard which allows for touch typing with only one hand. Pressing the space bar turns the left half of the keyboard into the right half and vice versa.

Another adaptive input device is the Magic Wand Keyboard, which provides full keyboard and mouse capability with the lightest touch of a wand. No strength or dexterity is required. This device enables disabled users to access the computer using standard software. It provides access with very limited one-handed movement or slight head movement and requires only a light touch and very little reach. A device such as this can make any computer accessible to the physically disabled without any special software or modification to the computer.

Voice recognition input is an option for individuals who are able to speak but are unable to physically access the computer using the keyboard or any of its adaptations. Appropriate alternate input devices enable individuals with physical impairments to use the computer to access data, produce written documents and graphics, use educational programs, and access communication devices.

Individuals who have difficulty typing or who use switch or scanning input can benefit from specialized software, such as word prediction word processing programs, which use artificial intelligence to try to predict which word a user is entering from only the first few letters of the word. Some standard word processing programs have word prediction as a built-in feature. There are also stand-alone word prediction programs that can be set up and used with any standard word processing program.

Individuals who have physical disabilities can also experience the fun of playing games through the use of adaptive devices. Using software such as Interaction Games published by Don Johnston Developmental Equipment, Inc., children and adults who have never played a game before can interact with others through the computer. With software such as *Pie in the Eye*, players can participate in a simulation of throwing pies at one another using a switch input device (Figure 4.1). When necessary, the game's parameters can be adjusted so a child with severe physical disabilities can interact with a non-handicapped child in a competitive situation. Children who have never been able to play a game before can hit a switch to throw a pie at their on-screen opponent, or hit a switch to have

Figure 4.1. The computer program, Pie in the Eye, from Don Johnston, Inc. provides an opportunity for individuals with physical disabilities to interact with their peers in a game-like situation. Photo courtesy of Don Johnston, Incorporated.

their on-screen self bend down to avoid being hit by their opponent's pie. Switch input devices can also be used for computer simulated games such as bowling and baseball.

Technology can also provide individuals with physical disabilities the satisfaction of creating through the arts. Children whose experience creating pictures has been limited to watching someone else make things for them, can now create their own art using the computer. Commercially distributed software such as Monsters and Make Believe and Best Fishes, both published by Pelican Software, and Creature Antics, published by Laureate, can be adapted for switch input using a switch interface or a board such as the Adaptive Firmware Card.

Examples of specific software and hardware become out-dated very quickly. What is important to take into account is how these various devices and the software that supports them can change the day-to-day experiences of an individual with disabilities through the enabling process. The extent to which adaptive technology can effectively enable an individual who is physically impaired can be seen in the case of Lauren Matur.

Lauren Matur: A Case Study of Adaptive Technology for An Individual with Physical Impairments

Lauren Matur is a twenty-seven-year old-woman who was seriously injured in an automobile accident when she was nineteen years old. She suffered a spinal cord injury at the third and fourth vertebrae, which resulted in her being para-lyzed from her shoulders down. After the accident she was on a respirator for two-and-a-half months. At the time of her acci-dent, Lauren had completed her first year of college at St. Lawrence University in Canton, New York. Two years after the accident, she resumed her studies and completed a degree in economics.

Lauren came to Miami to get help from the Miami Project, which is an experimental research program to develop more effective treatments for spinal cord injuries, based at the University of Miami Medical School. With extensive therapy, she has regained limited use of her right arm, and has limited tricep movement in her left arm. When we interviewed Lauren, she was partially strapped into her wheelchair. Despite the severity of her injury, she was able to function and operate with a large degree of independence because of adaptive technology.

Lauren works for a printing company as a telemarketer. She has a headpiece, which enables her to use a light-pointer as the input device for her computer. When using her computer, she selects a key and activates it by shining her light-pointer on an electronic/light sensitive keyboard. Included with her computer is a modem and an automatic dialing program. She explains how it works in the following way: "On my computer there is a dial program...All I have to do is hit D on my com-puter and it dials the number for me. Then I hit H for hang-up." In addition, Lauren has a tape recorder that can be activated by means of a switch, which allows her a backup system when she is taking addresses or orders. Later she types up her orders using her light-pointer. If the order is a simple one, she often takes it down using the light-pointer while she is still talking to the customer on the phone.

Lauren works almost completely out of her house. "I have a Lazy-Boy (reclining chair) and I can tip off on my side, which is another advantage of my keyboard because you don't have to sit straight up. Like, I can do it sort of on my side."

Lauren explained in her interview, that if it were not for adaptive technology, she would not have any way of financially supporting herself. Essentially, the computer and the special input devices she uses with it, make it possible for her to work as a sales person. Older technologies, such as a mouth stick used with an electric typewriter would not work for someone like Lauren because of being too slow, but even more importantly as Lauren explains: "You'd have to sit up straight to use the mouth stick, and you couldn't hold a stick in your mouth and talk at the same time."

Lauren wants to go back to college and get a master's degree in accounting. She is confident that she can do whatever work is necessary, not only for the degree but as a practicing accountant, with the help of adaptive computer technology. According to Lauren: "Nothing can stop you once you've got a computer."

VISUAL IMPAIRMENT

Visual impairment includes blindness, meaning that the individual is totally without sight or with so little sight that he or she must learn through the senses, and low vision, which is defined as follows:

> ...a level of vision that with standard correction hinders an individual in the visual planning and execution of tasks, but which permits enhancement of the functional vision through the use of optical aids and environmental modifications and/or techniques.[2]

Additional vision problems occur in individuals with severe motor impairments who are unable to hold their heads still enough to read printed materials. Adaptive technology for visually impaired individuals includes enlarging the size of visual materials, or transforming printed information into either a tactile or an auditory format. This is accomplished by using video enlarging devices, magnification software, large ink print, braille print, paperless braille, tactual output devices, and speech output. These devices have been described in detail in chapter 3.

Video enlarging devices include closed circuit television, large print display processors and computer image-enlarging systems. These devices are aids for individuals with low vision, who cannot access newspaper- and book-sized print without the aid of an enlarging system. Large print is also often appropriate for individuals with limited vision. Large print can be created using word processing programs capable of producing changes in font sizes along with printers that can print using large type formats.

Braille print is used by individuals who cannot benefit from enlarged print and is produced using braille printers. Braille is read by an individual using the sense of touch. Paperless braille involves the generation of braille text on a refreshable display system—one which typically raises braille text by electromagnetic processes.

Tactual output devices use a scanning device and a tactual array of vibrating rods to allow blind individuals access to the printed word. Using the computer and a tactual output device, a blind individual can access various data bases and other sources of information.

Speech output is the single most widely used computer adaptation for the visually impaired. Some speech output is produced using only software and the built-in sound capabilities of the computer, while other speech output requires additional hardware (Figure 4.2).

In addition to the adaptive output devices described above, voice input and optical character recognition systems are promising input devices for individuals who are visually impaired (Figure 4.3). Using voice input to control the computer—a technology still in the process of evolving—an individual who is visually impaired can bypass traditional graphic

Figure 4.2. The Screenreader from IBM enables people who are blind or visually impaired to hear the words that are displayed on the computer screen. Photo courtesy of EduQuest.

Figure 4.3. OsCaR from TeleSensory is an optical character reader system, which allows blind and visually impaired individuals to read print material without assistance. It is designed to be used with TeleSensory's large print, speech, electronic braille, or hard copy braille output devices. Photo courtesy of TeleSensory.

and text interfaces which he cannot see. The combination of scanning systems with voice output can serve as readers for the blind. A totally integrated system can scan any text, recognize voice commands, and provide output either in the form of the spoken word or braille.

The use of icons, or more accurately graphical user interfaces (GUI) has been a major development in the evolution of computers. Macintosh computers have always used a graphics-based operating system. More recently Microsoft Windows, a graphical interface system for MS-DOS computers, has come into widespread use and graphics-based operating systems are currently being developed by all major manufacturers of computers. These graphics-based operating systems are characterized by the use of icons to represent various functions and a mouse for pointing and control.

Research has confirmed that graphical user interface systems make it easier for sighted users to learn to use the computer. However its dependence on vision, makes the graphical user interface system inaccessible for individuals with visual impairments. Currently there are several research and development efforts directed toward making GUIs accessible to the blind.

Traditional screen reading programs do not work with GUIs, therefore an interception-based strategy has been developed which captures text information before it gets to the screen. Interception-based software is able to recognize and track the icons created by a GUI system and to provide audio-based information about the icon. This software also recognizes and tracks information about the text itself, such as fonts and formatting, which can also be conveyed to a visually impaired user through speech output.

Examples of this type of software include OutSPOKEN for the Macintosh, which provides blind individuals access to the Macintosh computer graphical user interface systems. Access to the Windows graphical user interface system is provided by programs such as Slimware Window Bridge, which uses a speech synthesizer to provide verbal information about the screen and WinVision from Artic Technologies.

The goal of access systems is to enable blind individuals to benefit from all the features of GUI on all computers. This has not yet been accomplished but major research and development efforts are underway to provide the full benefits of GUI to the blind.

The extent to which CD-ROM technology is having a profound impact in terms of enabling visually impaired individuals can be seen in some of the current systems available at the Cleveland Public Library.[3] CD-ROMs are providing the library's 11,000 blind and physically impaired patrons with information such as encyclopedia articles, consumer information, and materials from sources such as the *Physicians Desk Reference*. Information encoded on the CD-ROM in ASCII is printed in braille for the blind or in bold-faced type and large print size for individuals with limited vision. In addition, data can be read aloud by a speech synthesizer. References such as *The*

World Almanac, American Heritage Dictionary, Bartlett's Familiar Quotations, and *Roget's Thesaurus* are on CD-ROM and can therefore be accessed by the visually impaired in the form of braille, enlarged print, or the spoken word. The use of adaptive technology by an individual who is visually impaired can be seen in the case of Carrie Seigenthaler.

Carrie Seigenthaler: A Case Study of Adaptive Technology for an Individual Who is Visually Impaired

Carrie Seigenthaler is twenty-six-years of age and lives in the San Francisco area. Her use of adaptive technology has had a major impact on her life in terms of her ability to function independently and effectively in mainstream society. Her story suggests the importance of computer technology in enabling people like herself, as well as the problems involved in its implementation.

After graduating from California State University at Long Beach with a bachelor's degree in Psychology, Carrie went to work as a production assistant at the naval post-graduate school in Monterrey, California. At the time of her interview with us, she was not working, and was married to a sighted man who she met in high school and who was a lieutenant in the United States Navy.

Carrie attended kindergarten at the local elementary school near where she lived. From first through sixth grade she went to a school that had a classroom for the visually impaired. As she recalls:

> Like every other child, I had a regular classroom; but at any point in the day that I needed help, I could get up out of my chair and walk to the Itinerant Classroom or the Special Education Classroom. There wasn't any set time to go there; I could go there any time I wanted. I just had to tell my teacher that I was leaving, and I could get up and go. I usually did this about four or five times in a typical day. I would usually go into my regular classroom, get my assignment, take it to the itinerant room while the other kids were working on it in

the class, and I would either have the teacher there help me, or I would do it on a special machine called a Visual-Tek or have a teacher-aide assist me. Then, I would finish it, go back to the regular classroom, and then maybe they'd go on to spelling. I'd get the assignment and go back to the special education room. So I was just basically getting my assignments. I wasn't being taught by the regular teacher. I was being taught by the special education teacher.

In junior high, I went to the school that was near my house but it also happened to be the one in my district that had the special education room. So I could walk to school with my friends, and then again if I needed help I could go to that classroom at any time. I usually walked to the special ed room by myself because the times when I would go there were when the other kids were in class, so there weren't a lot of students to maneuver around. You just learned your way. In junior high school I very rarely used the special education room. I used people in the classes who sat next to me. And I learned that I could ask the teacher for help. Maybe once a day I'd go to the special education room, but not very often. Once the [regular] teachers understood that I was bright enough, that I was not going to drag all their time out of them and that I could pick up things, they were more than willing to help me. At first, when I asked different teachers, they'd say "Well, I can't give you all my time." When they finally understood that I didn't want all their time, only a few minutes, they were pretty good. At the beginning of the semester, they would ask the class who would be willing to sit next to me and do readings for extra credit. I remember in one history class that there were about five students who wanted the extra credit, so I let each of them sit next to me for a day and I chose which one I wanted to sit next to me for the whole semester, whoever was the more literate.

In high school, the special education classroom was at a different location and I didn't want to be bussed, so I went to the regular one near my house. I had an itinerant teacher, who would come in and work with me on anything that I needed. I would have one period in my schedule that was for that teacher to come in and work with me. If I didn't have anything that I needed to work on, we would work on my braille skills or homework.

In college, I would pick my own classes and go to Disabled Student Services with my schedule and coordinate with the Notetaker and Reader Service. These people were paid by them to take my notes and read whatever material I needed read. Another person was my test proxy, because it was against the rules to have the same person who was your notetaker be your test proxy. They might coach you if you chose the wrong answer or something. Disabled Student Services also had equipment that you could go in and use, like Visual-Teks, braille writers, typewriters. And in the library they had a whole computer center. It had what was then a huge machine called a Kurzweil Reader, which was something that would read printed material in a very computer-like voice. They also had computers with voice synthesizers and all sorts of adaptive equipment that dealt with computers.

While I was in college, I was Commissioner of Disabled Student Services. After I graduated, I started working as a live-in care person for a quadriplegic.

The very first memory I have of adaptive equipment in my education was in kindergarten. The itinerant teacher would come in and work with me, and I remember the way they taught me my letters. They used these six-by-six plastic cards that had three lines drawn across them like lines on a paper and then the letters drawn—capital and lower case—in what felt like sandpaper. So the plastic was smooth and the letters and lines were made of this sandpaper, and that's how they taught me my letters. I remember thinking "Why is this important? I'm never going to see them. I'm never going to write them. I'm going to use braille." I remember, even at five, thinking it was so stupid. The thought of this curvy line being an "S" and representing something important. Not seeing it in context or reading it in a book representing, say, "spot", didn't make sense to me. I remember fighting with the teacher, asking "Why do I need to learn these letters? I can't see them!" Now, I think thank goodness they fought back and made me do it because now at least I have the concept of writing. If I have to print, I can. If I had never learned writing it would probably be very difficult for me now.

In second grade, they started teaching all the visually impaired kids how to type because they knew that your writing would most likely be illegible, so they teach you very early how to type. They have smaller typewriters because your fingers are littler. I remember learning how to write cursive writing on this thing that looked like a window screen. You wrote on a paper with a crayon, and it made a texture where you wrote. Then, you could feel what you wrote. So it would teach you how to sign your name and write by feeling it. We learned how to read using the Visual-Tek, and it was really difficult because you could only fit about three letters on the screen. A lot of times you couldn't get the whole word. Not seeing the whole word is really hard. People usually see whole words in order to identify them. In math, instead of writing the problems vertically, we did a lot of work with abacuses to learn the concepts. We did a lot of math that way and with blocks, because the visual part of numbers was so hard. I remember having these big tactile maps on the wall to learn geography. Those are the big things I remember from elementary school.

In junior high, it was the phase in my life when I didn't want people to know that I couldn't see, so I didn't want to use the special equipment. I would go to the visually-impaired room, and I would use the

Visual-Tek if I absolutely had to. I preferred to be read to. Then it wasn't as noticeable.

My sight was also getting worse, so the Visual-Tek was harder to use. When I was in about eighth or ninth grade they tried to teach me to use a machine called an Octagon. It's a machine that looks like a tape recorder. In the front it has a slot where your fingers fit on one hand. On your other hand you hold a camera about the size of a cigarette lighter, and you run it across the printed page. It conveys the image of each letter over to these sensors that your fingers are on, making the shape of each letter. You can't read anything other than print, and it's very difficult. I remember thinking "What a god-awful way to learn to read!" I'd rather listen to a tape any day than do this. That didn't last too long.

In high school, there was a Visual-Tek in the library for when I needed it. I wouldn't use braille in my classes because I didn't want people to see me in my class using it. Again, I always had people in my class sit next to me and read to me or draw things on my hand if it was in my geometry class. There weren't any computers at that time that had been adapted or were affordable, so I didn't get to use them through high school.

In college, I used computers extensively. That's how I did research, wrote my papers. The computer I have now has voice synthesized output, with a voice card. It also comes with software. It's called "Artic Symphonic Speech." The package is called a screen reader, so anything that comes up on the screen I can access—except graphics. So if I'm on a mainframe, I can get into databases. I can use all my applications programs. In the last eight years, they've come up with these things that anybody who's visually impaired can use. They start anywhere from about six hundred dollars and go up to several thousand dollars. It's just a matter of preference: the type of voice you prefer, the kind of needs you have. I don't know how I made it before.

I'm so dependent on my computer now. Before when I would type, like in junior high, there was no way of knowing if I'd made a mistake. And now with the computer that's all alleviated.

At work at the navy, they didn't provide me with any adaptive equipment and that's why I'm in litigation right now. I had to supply my own equipment. I took the voice card out of my computer at home and brought it in to work. I made the phone calls to Honeywell Computers to find out how I could access the main computers. I had to get a terminal emulator program from them to make my IBM voice card compatible with their system. I spoke to a man who was very helpful and turned out to be a vice president. I took in my braille writer from home. It isn't a small machine, so each day I had to lug it back and forth between home and work. Also, I had to talk to the phone repairman from public works to figure how out to adapt the phone lines coming in on the switchboard. Since I couldn't see the lights of the phone lines I was supposed to be answering, I didn't know which one was ringing. We adapted it by giving each line a different tone, so then I could answer the phones no matter where I was in the office. I wasn't stuck to just my phone. Finally, we adapted the copy machine by sticking plastic labeling on the copy machine so that I could feel where to put papers to be xeroxed.

I am suing them right now for discrimination because I had to fight for everything I needed to make my work place adaptable. At one point, during a performance appraisal by my boss, he informed me that he wouldn't promote me until I could do every aspect of my job by myself. He was basically saying that until I could read, he wouldn't promote me. When I would ask a co-worker what a piece of mail said, he wouldn't allow that and he wouldn't designate someone to be a reader for me.

Looking back, I'd have to say the adaptive tools that made me more "mainstreamed" were the

ones that helped me learn how to write: learning
my letters the way I did, learning braille. The tools
that I could use other places and were portable
were the best. It's great to learn things like the computer, if you can afford it. But there are so many
things that are so unaffordable. It's almost useless
to learn those things if you can't afford them. It's a
waste of your time. The things I could take and use
most readily were things like tapes, more so than
working on my reading skills because I couldn't
transport that easily—I couldn't read wherever I
was because I had to have a Visual-Tek, and I
couldn't carry that around.

If some of the latest developments in technology had been available, they would have helped me
especially in the area of reading and spelling. I
never knew how to spell because I never saw whole
words, so now my spelling is horrible; but with the
computer, because I'm writing with it and spelling
with it, it's the first time I've ever been able to see
my mistakes. It's a great tool. In creative writing, it
helps you, rather than someone else editing your
work. It makes a big difference. When you can see
and correct your own mistakes, you really learn.
The Kurzweil Personal Reader would also have
been a great help. It only weighs about fourteen
pounds and folds out like a lap top printer or copier.
You lay out the book on this piece of plexiglass and
the copier reads it. You hear this wonderful voice.
That, in itself, would have opened up the library to
me. I could have been a part of the class. And I
could have used an earphone, so I wouldn't have
had to disturb the class. When the other kids were
learning to read and comprehend, I could have
been a part of that process instead of always having
to leave and go to the resource room. I remember
as a little kid going to the library, going through the
sections, and picking out books that I wish I could
read. I would take them home and tell everyone
that I read them. I never really read them, but I
wanted to so bad. I would just take them back to

school and tell them I read them. At home they didn't have the time to read them all to me; but if I had had the personal reader, I could have read them. Now, there are a lot of books that are on tape, but not everything is. You have to wait usually two to three years from when something comes out [as a book] and when it comes out on tape. Tapes are nice, but that personal reader opens up a lot. But they're about ten to twelve thousand dollars each. There are loans available for lower-income people, but if you're above the poverty level you can't get the loan. You can't lease them or borrow them. I've done a lot of research. You can get loans at the standard 18% rates.

The resources, then, for getting these adaptive devices are: save your money. There are some programs, though. There is a program that the Department of Social Security has called PASS, or Plan to Achieve Self-Sufficiency. If you're putting money into an account to buy something like the Kurzweil Personal Reader, say, they will match that dollar for dollar, as long as you are putting into savings. It's a great program as long as you qualify for Social Security. I don't because I'm married, but I know a lot of people who are doing it. The other source is that every state has some form of a Department of Rehabilitation. They are there to help disabled persons achieve some sort of self-sufficiency, whether it's vocational training or what. They will most of the time help you get through college. My whole college education was paid through them. They pay for books, tuition, everything. And then when you go to work, if you need a computer or voice synthesizer to make you employable, they will buy you that. And once you're employed for six months, you're no longer a client of theirs. They've done their job: they've made you employable. A friend of mine lost one of her legs, so they got her a prosthetic leg to help make her employable.

There are organizations for the visually impaired like the American Foundation for the Junior

Blind and another national organization that can help you find where the loans are. But there again, they are usually high-interest loans, because they're all signature loans. While I was commissioner of Disabled Student Services at my college, I learned a lot about writing grants to get money; but most of what I know I've picked up from talking to other blind people. They don't have a book out that tells you where everything's at, or at least I've never seen one. A lot of things are nice little secrets because people don't want to share them. They're afraid you'll take the money that they're entitled to. Like the loans they had out to get the Kurzweil Readers with, they were through the Bank of Boston. I called six different places where I knew the people would know, but they don't want to tell anyone because only a certain number of people can get these loans. So they don't want any more people to apply for them. Because money is so scarce, people are very cutthroat.

When I think of the most pressing needs in exceptional education today, I think people should understand that the kids need to be made as much a part of their classes as they can be—not to be treated any more special than any other children. It's important to give them the help that they need, but also to teach them that they can supply their own help—to teach them how to ask for help and how to use their resources. It's important to build their self-esteem—to tell them that "Yes, you are disabled," or "Yes, you are impaired in some way, but it's not going to stop you." Building their self-esteem and self-respect is what's going to get them through. There are going to be so many people in their lives trying to tear them down that if they can build themselves up psychologically, they can get through anything. And as I said before, it's important to teach them to ask for help—that asking is not bad. A lot of kids are afraid to ask because people have said no. And if someone does say no, they simply go and ask someone else and not worry about it. Kids need to be involved. So what if they bump their knees more than anyone else when they're playing out on the playground? And so what if they get hurt a little? It's just going to toughen them up, and they need to be tough because they're going to get a lot more bumps out in the world.

If I had to describe the ideal physical setting for, say, a visually impaired first-grader today, first off, and this may sound trivial, let the child choose where he or she wants to sit. I was always put in the very front row in the right corner, and I hated it! I was stuck in my little corner, and no one was supposed to disrupt it. Let the kid decide where he's comfortable—where he belongs in that room. The ideal would be to have a teacher's aide or an itinerant teacher or somebody come in at set times in the day who would come in and help: at reading time, math time, etc. Have them sit next to him— not take him out of the room. Or even have them off in a corner of the room, so they wouldn't disturb everyone. But have them in the room so the others could see that he isn't some weird animal— that he's doing the same thing they are, that he's just doing it a little differently. Have all the tools, the technology in the room. If several students in the school have to share the equipment, pick one day to take all the students in that child's class to show them the special room where the equipment is, so they know where that child will be going. Then they won't have that feeling "Well, where is he going? Why is he so special?" Let them see what it is, how those things work, and that student does those things. Involve them, so they know what's going on. The idea of mainstreaming is wonderful, but they are defeating the purpose when they mainstream them and then pull them out of their classrooms. I understand teachers are pressed. They have forty students in a classroom, but if they can give them a teacher's aide or give them a few minutes of their time and start them on their way, they'd be fine.

If I could get them the best tools, I would defi-
nitely say a computer with a voice synthesizer and
probably a Kurzweil Reader. Again, I wouldn't
throw away those old tools they used twenty years
ago with me for learning how to do handwriting on
the screen or the sandpaper for learning the letters.
I don't know if any new ways of doing that are any
better, but I would make sure they know those
basic skills too. A Kurzweil Reader is wonderful,
but there are some basic things they also need to
know—to have a picture of how to write in the
backs of their minds....

Carrie's interview provides an idea of what it was like to
progress through the public educational system in California in
the 1970s and '80s as a visually impaired person. Her comments
make it clear that while adaptive technology is of critical importance to educating people like herself, the human and financial
support systems provided to her were equally important.

CONCLUSION

The use of adaptive technology for individuals who are
physically or visually impaired, represents a particularly exciting use of computer technology. Individuals who are severely
limited physically or visually, but who function normally in
other regards, can now be enabled through the use of various
technologies. Both the cases of Lauren and Carrie provide
excellent examples of individuals who can now be gainfully
employed and more actively involved in a range of different
activities and experiences because of creative uses of adaptive
technology. It is worth reflecting for a moment on what both of
these women's lives would be like without this technology.
Certainly each of them would be more financially dependent
upon others, as well as less socially independent. In turn each
would probably not have as strong a sense of self-esteem if the
possibilities provided by adaptive technology were not available
to them.

Potential further developments in the use of adaptive technology with physically and visually impaired individuals is almost unlimited. Adaptive technologies can provide individuals with physical disabilities the opportunity to lead richer and more productive lives. For the visually impaired, they can provide important alternative ways of communicating with and sensing, as well as decoding, the world.

5

ADAPTIVE TECHNOLOGY
AND THE
SPEECH AND HEARING IMPAIRED

Communication is one of the fundamental characteristics of
human beings. All individuals have the need to communicate.
Being able to do so provides a means to assert oneself as an
individual, ask questions, test concepts, express and elicit feelings, and participate in play. By communicating we are able to
develop social, emotional and cognitive competence and a
sense of control.

SPEECH IMPAIRMENT

Individuals may be pre-verbal or non-verbal because of
mild to severe physical disabilities, developmental delays,
developmental apraxia (the inability to perform coordinated
movements as a result of lesions in the cerebral cortex), oral
motor difficulties, and other language impairments. Many
people who are unable to speak are also unable to write or
even to make their wishes known through facial expressions
and gestures. This can be as a result of a stroke, cerebral palsy,
head or spinal injuries, or can be associated with mental retardation or a degenerative disorder such as Lou Gehrig's disease.
It is critical for individuals with problems such as these to augment their ability to communicate.

Speech impairment includes problems such as difficulty
with articulation or voice, stuttering, or language disorders.

For individuals who have hearing and speech impairments, computer-based speech output devices can demonstrate how to correctly pronounce and articulate words. Deaf individuals can speak words using voice input and see the representation of their speech on a computer display.

Augmentative communication refers to communication that supplements or augments speech, and is used by individuals who are not able to communicate orally. It embodies a wide range of methods that are used to help people communicate, ranging from very simple to complex systems. These can include behaviors, gestures, or manual sign languages.

Communication can be assisted through many assorted devices. Aided communication is the use of systems or devices that are external to the user. The extent of available methods to aid communication is indicated by the fact that the Crestwood Company's catalog of communication aids includes 228 different devices for persons of all ages who have limited communication capabilities. These systems can be categorized as follows: (1) No-tech, which are non-electronic systems or devices such as picture communication boards, picture folders, or eye gaze activities; (2) Low-tech, which include simple electronic systems or devices such as dial scanners, clock communicators, or mini card readers (Figure 5.1); and (3) High-tech, which are sophisticated electronic devices including dedicated communication systems and computer systems programmed to provide communication capabilities (Figures 5.2 and 5.3).

Individuals can communicate ideas through vocalizations, word approximations, gestures, facial expressions, sign language, written output, pointing to pictures or symbols, eye movement, scanning or speech production devices. Pictures alone do not always furnish enough meaning, but when combined with prerecorded speech or synthesized speech can provide a better connection to spoken language.

Computers play a crucial role with high-technology aided communication devices. More specifically, for individuals with speech disabilities, these devices can provide two types of assistance: a means to communicate, and a means to teach proper speech and provide feedback on speech production.

The computer and related technologies enable pre-verbal or non-verbal individuals to communicate, which leads to many other aspects of functioning in society. Synthesized

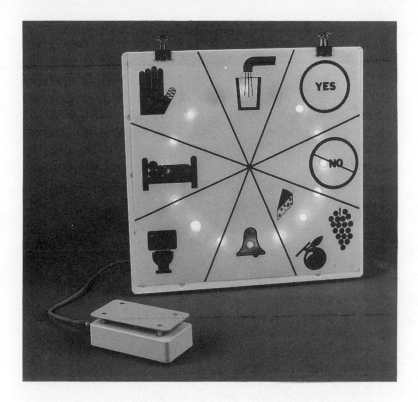

Figure 5.1. Versascan from Prentke Romich is an aid for individuals with limited communication needs. It allows an individual to scan and select from a circular array of choices using a single switch. Photo courtesy of Prentke Romich.

speech functions as a voice for individuals, letting them name objects and events and make their wants and needs known. Users can have words repeated many times and imitate them. Computers with synthesized speech can provide the experience of using both spoken and written language. The computer acts as a scaffold for language, supporting its use in order to communicate meaning while developing language skills. Speech output must be under the complete control of the

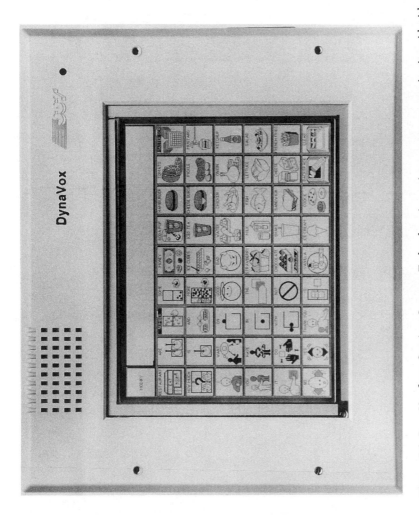

Figure 5.2. DynaVox from Sentient Systems Technology is a voice output communication aid with a graphic display and speech output. It may be accessed by touch, single and dual switch scanning, joystick, or mouse. Because of its intuitive language-based architecture, it is relatively easy to learn to use. Photo courtesy of Sentient Systems Technology, Inc.

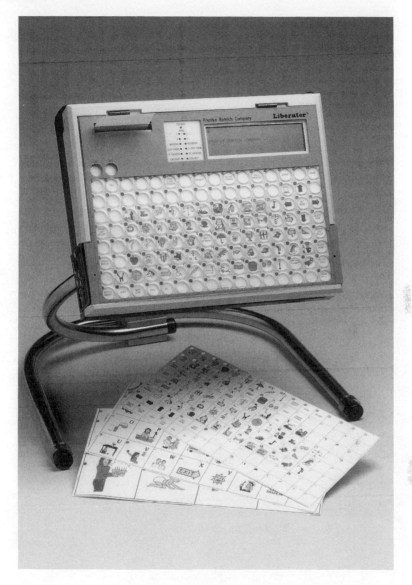

Figure 5.3. The Liberator from Prentke Romich provides high quality
speech synthesis with age and gender appropriate voices. It is a writing
tool that can be used as an alternate keyboard to most computers and it
can operate environmental controls. It also provides audible scanning and
menus for people with visual impairments. Photo courtesy of Prentke
Romich.

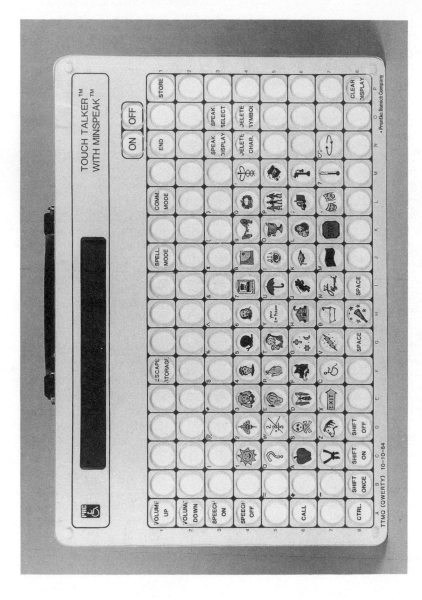

Figure 5.4. The Touch Talker from Prentke Romich. Courtesy of Prentke Romich.

individual. Using a device that produces prerecorded speech or synthesized speech is especially helpful for children who are able to understand language at a higher level than they can produce.

A variety of portable speech output devices are available for aided communication. Known as Voice Output Communication Aids (VOCAs), these are often referred to as dedicated speech devices. Selecting the most appropriate speech output device is a complicated process and is usually done in consultation with one or more professionals.

Devices are currently available that are based on a large number of technologies that have various levels of complexity and use. The Touch Talker, for example, consists of 128 touch-sensitive keys that can be custom programmed on a small display (Figure 5.4). Additional overlays are available to provide larger and fewer activation points. The Touch Talker can be hooked to a printer or used as an input device connected to a computer. Another aided communication device is the Light Talker, a portable speech synthesis device that utilizes scanning with single or multiple switches or an optical head pointer (Figure 5.5). SpeechPac is built around a portable Epson computer, has sixty-eight keys and stores messages using logical letter coding, so a letter code must be remembered for each message. EvalPac is an expanded version of the SpeechPac with additional input modes including scanning, the Unicorn Board and an optical head pointer.

A much less expensive system than the ones described above is the Wolf, which is a commonly used voice output communication aid (Figures 5.6 and 5.7). The Wolf is for users able to use a touch panel or it can be adapted for scanning and single switch selection. The Wolf is a multi-level device, meaning it allows more than one message to be stored under each key or activation point; messages are assigned to different levels like different pages stacked one on top of the other. The user can flip through levels or pages to retrieve a desired message. The Wolf holds up to 475 words on a maximum of thirty pages. The advantages of the Wolf are its low cost, sturdy construction and portability.

Augmentative communication technology, which includes both hardware and software options, is rapidly changing. New types of hardware and software are constantly becoming available. Factors to consider when choosing Voice Output

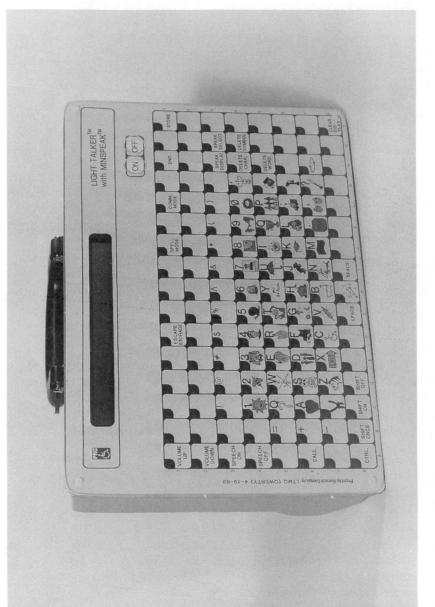

Figure 5.5. The Light Talker from Prentke Romich. Photo courtesy of Prentke Romich.

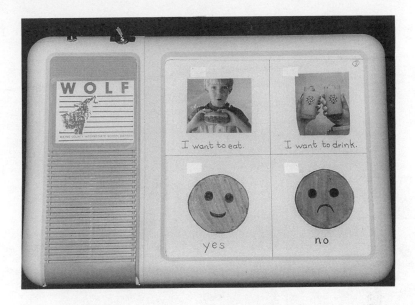

Figure 5.6. Wolf photo courtesy of Wayne County Regional Educational Service Agency/ADAMLAB.

Communication Aids include: (*a*) voice (intelligibility, gender availability, pitch, volume), (*b*) input methods, (*c*) memory, (*d*) ability to program, (*e*) symbol flexibility, (*f*) visual output, (*g*) portability, (*h*) cost, and (*i*) computer access.

Alternative computer input devices such as the PowerPad, TouchWindow, and Unicorn Board can be programmed as talking communication boards using a speech synthesizer. Presently the disadvantage of most computers as communication devices is that they are not easily portable, although the potential for true portability is becoming greater with laptop and notebook-sized computers. Using these programmable alternative computer input devices, children can participate in areas of the curriculum such as math and science by using overlays that are appropriate for each subject. In developing overlays, vocabulary should obviously be appropriate to the content being taught. General phrases should be used as much

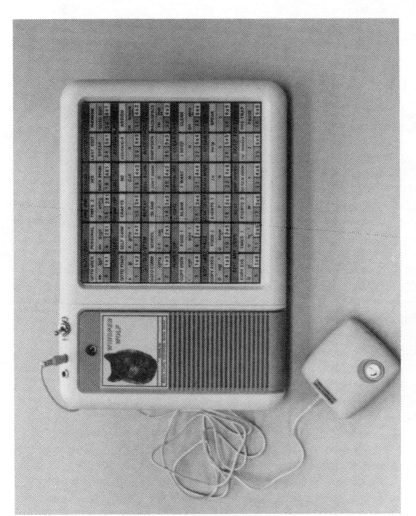

Figure 5.7. Whisper Wolf is a user-programmable Wolf that provides auditory scanning and selection either by switch or touch panel. Photo courtesy of Wayne County Regional Educational Service Agency/ADAMLAB.

as possible, so the overlay will not have to be completely redone every day. Phrases should be included that will allow questions and that include such responses as "Yes," "No," "I don't know," and "I don't understand."

Voice output communication devices can be programmed in interesting and creative ways. For example, children love to tell jokes and they go through various stages of what is funny to them. Non-verbal children can experience telling jokes using the Wolf or other similar types of communication devices. In a classroom, the teacher can set aside time for comedy when one or more children can wear a funny wig or hat, get a microphone, and tell a joke using their communication devices. Two Wolfs can be programmed with knock, knock or similar types of responsive jokes so two children can do a routine. Children can even put on a play using communication systems to say their lines and sing songs, or overlays can be made to enable a non-verbal student to tell a story to a group of children. The Unicorn, PowerPad or other devices can be set up to give instructions for activities so that a non-verbal individual can direct other children in some physical activity. Commands such as turn around, clap your hands, or all fall down can be programmed on the communication board and can provide a child with disabilities an opportunity to engage in shared experiences, fun, and activities at a level not previously possible.

Computers with voice recognition systems can assist in training people with speech impairments. For example, software produced by Ani-Vox has a program in which the user must make a specific sound correctly in order to move a figure across a screen.

SpeechStation is a speech analysis system from Ariel Corporation that is designed for IBM and compatible computers. It accepts input from a microphone or tape recorder and provides recording and playback, waveform editing, and the comparison of speech segments. Spectograms can be displayed and printed, and the user can compare the vocalizations of two different speakers or the same utterance by the same person at two different times.

IBM's SpeechViewer uses a microphone and a computer to digitize sounds made by an individual (Figure 5.8). The computer evaluates the speech and gives feedback on various

Figure 5.8. The IBM SpeechViewer is designed to increase the efficiency of speech therapy and speech modification by converting elements of speech acoustics to interactive graphic displays. Photo courtesy of EduQuest.

speech characteristics such as pitch, voicing, loudness, and timing. Devices such as this are of tremendous value for speech pathologists attempting to help individuals who have serious speech limitations. Such systems provide remarkable possibilities for individuals who have suffered strokes or other injuries to the brain.

Programs such as Panasonic's computerized speech training system, which uses sensors, training software and computerized graphics, can assist the hearing impaired in mastering pronunciation. The system's computer monitor first displays a model or graphic pattern of a correct vocalization of one of eight different parameters of speech. The user then vocalizes and tries to recreate the displayed pattern. The software measures the vocalization and graphically displays it on the monitor for instant visual feedback. Without benefit of hearing, the user can tell if his or her pronunciation is correct.[1]

Technology is also being used to help aphasics. Usually caused by stroke or head trauma, aphasia is a condition in which the individual has difficulty using language. This condition can range in severity from the inability to recall a word, to complete inability to read, write, speak, or understand spoken language. Lingraphica is a graphical language, developed for use on the Macintosh computer, which enables individuals with aphasia to communicate more effectively by linking icons representing words and concepts into complete ideas and sentences.[2]

Some software available for speech and language acquisition is not only designed for individuals with speech problems, but also for those with limited English proficiency. For example, in Florida a curriculum called Technology Assisted Language Learning Project is being developed. Networking, CD-ROM, language learning labs, and videodisc technology will be used in teaching English to Speakers of Other Languages (ESOL).[3] Laureate Learning Systems has developed a series of programs for language development.[4] In this series, several stages of language development have been identified and software appropriate for instructional intervention has been created at each of these stages. One such program, First Verbs, combines moving pictures and synthesized speech to teach forty frequently occurring verbs (Figure 5.9). Each verb is illustrated by two pictures and spoken by a speech synthesizer. First Categories teaches classification of nouns and

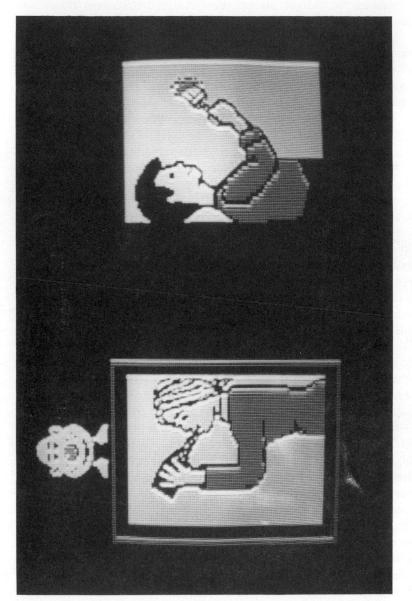

Figure 5.9. First Verbs. Photo courtesy of Laureate Learning Systems, Incorporated.

Words and Concepts, integrates language and concept training. Peal also has several programs designed for early language acquisition. Programs such as Keytalk, Exploratory Play and Representational Play, authored by Laura Meyers, provide graphics and synthesized speech and use the Muppet keyboard as an input device. These types of programs provide children who have major speech problems with a synthesized voice. Such programs also help children understand the sound patterns of the English language by providing them with the means to listen to an individual word as many times as they need.

The case of Mike Morgan shows how technology can provide the bridge necessary for establishing communication. Mike has multiple disabilities: he is cognitively limited, physically impaired, and is unable to speak.

Mike Morgan: A Case Study of Adaptive Technology and Its Use with an Individual with Multiple Disabilities

Mike Morgan is a fourteen-year-old boy who has cerebral palsy. Born three months premature, his birth weight was less than two pounds. He is currently in the eighth grade, but looks only about seven or eight years of age. Mike is a quadriplegic and is unable to produce speech. He is an attractive child, who has a charming disposition and an obvious sense of humor.

Mike's first school experience was in the first grade of a special education center, the Quest School, which is part of the Broward County Public Schools. When he entered the Quest School, Mike was classified as profoundly mentally handicapped. He was reevaluated after the second grade, and his classification was changed to educable mentally handicapped. From our interview with Mike, we felt that he probably had a higher level of intellectual function than what was indicated by his psychological assessment. For example, he clearly understood when we were talking about him, when jokes were made, and, using his Light Talker communication device, frequently interjected himself into the flow of what was going on. It is very difficult, however, to assess just how much Mike is capable of learning, given his lack of speech capability and his inability to control his movement.

Our interview was conducted with his mother, Penny Barile, and Beth Sanders, the technology resource teacher who works with Mike at the Quest Center. Mike has almost no control over his movements. He uses a headswitch connected to a Light Talker operating in scanning mode to communicate. The Light Talker has rows and columns of symbols that represent words, phrases or sentences, which have been programmed into the device. In the scanning mode, a light moves across the Light Talker's symbols and Mike activates them using a head switch. A synthesized voice pronounces the words that have been programmed for that part of the board. The Light Talker can be programmed in several layers or successive screens. As a result, Mike can switch from one screen to another and greatly expand the words or phrases available to him.

Programmed onto Mike's Light Talker are words like "Yes" and "No," as well as useful phrases like "I'm hungry," "Hello, my name is Mike." and even jokes and riddles. For example, when we were interviewing him, Mike told us, using the Light Talker, his favorite riddle, which was "Why do you have to wear boots at the pet store?" "Because you might step in a poodle."

Mike has recently begun to use his headswitch to activate Apple II computer programs. Using the scanning mode of the computer he is able to type in his name and do simple cause and effect and matching activities. In addition, he is able to play very simple competitive race games that require him to choose numbers with the greatest potential value as they move by him in a scanning mode. Using this simple race game, Mike is able to participate in play and game activities with other people, despite the fact that the only movement over which he has control is that of his head.

Besides participating in educational programs and games on the Apple II computer, Mike plays a specially adapted version of Nintendo's Super Mario Brothers 2, in which he can use his head switch to move the characters in the game—making them jump and shoot. Using adaptive technology to access games on the Apple II and Nintendo systems has opened a whole world of play and interaction that previously had not been available to Mike. As simulations become increasingly adapted for use in special education settings, it will be interesting to see the extent to which they expand the experience and worlds of children such as Mike. One can imagine, for example, him working with a game like SimCity in which he is able to control the activities of a complex city in terms of resources, environment, and other factors. Although such a program might be too difficult for him, it suggests the types of models that could be simplified and adapted for his use.

Mike poses unique problems in terms of his making maximum use of the possibilities provided by adaptive technology. His multiple limitations make establishing a "bridge" or "link" to him much more difficult. Essentially, he has needs in several areas and does not fit into any single category of disability. In turn, he and others like him need access to multiple types of technology in order to gain the maximum benefit. Establishing communication was a critical first step in helping him, and had to be addressed before other areas, such as the development of cognitive skills, could be. With Mike's ability to access instructional computer programs through his headswitch, he is able for the first time to participate in educational activities.

HEARING IMPAIRMENT

Hearing impairment ranges from mild impairment, which includes hearing sounds faintly, hearing only certain frequencies and being unable to hear those sounds clearly, to profound deafness. Even the mildest hearing loss can decrease language development and ability to communicate. Therefore speech problems often accompany hearing impairment.

Individuals with hearing impairments have little difficulty using standard computer input and output devices, except when the output is sound only. However, the hearing impaired have problems understanding much of the information presented by typical educational software programs. Many of these individuals are fluent in American sign language, but have difficulty reading standard written English. The language and vocabulary found in many computer programs are too sophisticated for many hearing impaired individuals, who typically have problems with sentence structure and idiomatic use of English. However, if the language level of the software is appropriate for them, students with hearing impairments can use computers to help them develop language, writing and problem-solving skills.

Writing is a particularly difficult task for individuals with hearing impairments. These individuals typically make writing errors similar to those made by individuals whose first language is not English and errors caused by the difference between American Sign Language and written English. Their writing usually shows problems with verbs, missing words, and spelling errors. One piece of software developed specifically to help individuals with hearing impairments correct these errors is Write This Way, a processing program that checks spelling and grammar, from Interactive Learning Materials. This program has two versions: one designed for individuals with hearing impairments and the other for those with learning disabilities. It provides feedback on a variety of writing errors including spelling, capitalization, punctuation, grammar, and usage. The system detects errors and, when students request, can help them correct these errors. Specialized software such as this can help individuals with hearing impairments become more comfortable as well as more accurate writing standard English.

Computer software designed to develop English language skills can also be of value to individuals who are hearing impaired. Programs such as ESL Tutor from Disabled Programmers, Inc. is designed to improve the reading and writing skills of individuals whose primary language is American sign language.

Computers can be used to expand the learning environment of the hearing impaired in the same way that they do hearing students. They can help replace the typical verbal teaching of the regular classroom and can even be used to help teach sign language. Technology such as hypermedia, which is disussed in chapter 7, provides the capability to produce materials, at various language levels, which will be more effective for hearing-impaired students who may be delayed in their learning because of their disability.

Other technology, such as the PhoneCommunicator system developed by IBM, enables individuals with hearing and speech impairments to communicate by telephone. It presents dialogue as text on a computer screen, allowing individuals who are hearing impaired to hold conversations with anyone using a touch-tone phone and telecommunication devices for the deaf (TDD).[5]

Speech training systems mentioned in the previous section can be of tremendous value in helping deaf individuals learn to speak correctly. By seeing a graphic representation of their speech on the computer, they are able to judge how accurately they are producing speech.

Related to computer technologies for the deaf are systems such as the Maxon wireless microphone transmitter. This device transmits a lecture from an instructor directly to a student who is hearing impaired. It is much less conspicuous than a hearing aid and is more efficient. Vibrating beepers, flashing emergency alarms, and vibrating devices that act as alarm clocks are obviously practical and important devices, which we believe will be increasingly integrated into computer-based systems for the deaf. One example of a deaf individual using adaptive technology as a regular part of his life is that of John Paul Jebian.

John Paul Jebian: A Case Study of Adaptive Technology for an Individual Who Is Profoundly Deaf

John Paul Jebian is profoundly deaf. He is a twenty-one-year-old computer science major at Miami Dade Community College. He attends classes at the college three days a week, and has had a part-time job at the airport for the last six months. He describes his work as follows:

> At the airport I work with data entry in the marketing office. I check numbers and find mistakes. When I graduate I will use the experience from this job to help me get a job in computers.
>
> My boss told me that I could bring a TDD (a telecommunication device for the deaf) into the office for myself. I can have it at my desk and I can make calls. They do not provide one at work, but I wish they would.

According to the law, a TDD doesn't have to be provided by an employer for someone like John unless making telephone calls is part of his job description. John believes that enabling systems such as the TDD should be built into all telephone systems so that:

> Every deaf person would be able to use TDD all over with easy access if they have a touch tone phone. I'm hoping to have one of those computers in my workplace. The old system is almost archaic with too many people needing to use the service and not enough funding to provide adequate relay service so people get frustrated when they can't get through. They get a lot of busy signals, and it is an old system.

John was born in Venezuela and went to school in California and Miami. There were no programs for him in Venezuela: "No sign language, no hearing aids, nothing." His first experience in American schools was at the elementary level in an instructional class for the deaf.

> I had an old fashioned hearing aid—one that had a receiver that you wore around your neck. But it was always a problem. People would hit it...I ultimately changed to hearing aids on both ears and it eliminated the risk of people hitting my receiver. In school we also had flashing fire alarms for fire drills, but at the time still there wasn't very much technology. At that time they didn't have closed caption television so they had to interpret everything.

John goes on to describe how assistance was limited to an interpreter appearing at the bottom of the television screen in a small "bubble" or "window,"

> Interpreters on the bottom of the television screen was about it for technology. They would interpret at such an adult level. And the show was for little kids. I couldn't understand it. It wasn't until closed caption came along that I was able to start understanding. My father gave me a TV that had a special adapter. From then on it was different. I got used to watching TV finally. I became somewhat addicted

to it. Before when I watched television I had to constantly ask "What did they say?" And everybody got tired of me. Now I have my own TV in my own room. I don't have to bother anybody.

John found himself isolated in school because of his deafness.

In elementary school I was always with the deaf students. I wasn't with the hearing students. In junior high school, there was some mainstreaming going on. If I was with the hearing classes I needed to have an interpreter. Things constantly have been getting better since I was in elementary school. The government has really helped a whole lot....In elementary school they didn't have TDDs. They didn't know anything about technology. There was the technology out there, but it wasn't widely known— like alarms to get you up in the morning and things like that. But now they have all different kinds of alarms...telephones, doors, and you can answer your phone like everybody else.

John feels that sophisticated computer systems have some decided advantages for deaf individuals like himself over some of the more traditional TDD technology.

The TDD shows you one line at a time, but the computer is capable of allowing you to turn your attention away from the telephone while something is going on. If you want, you can look back and the conversation is all there. I don't want to get to the point where it is a jungle of technology. If it can be condensed and have a fewer number of machines available that's better....A computer should be able to do it all eventually. We should be able to have video on the screen and then we can just visually talk to the people we want to see. It is so much better than writing or calling because sign language is so visual. And when talking to hearing people, the computer will be able to transfer sign language into

words so that hearing people can understand us
and we can communicate with them.

John wants to see an expansion of services available for
deaf individuals.

They should be able to caption movies for hearing
impaired people. Without a closed caption you are
lost. Maybe one day of the week they would close
caption the movies for people, or there could be a
section of the theater where the caption could run
across the back of the chairs. I heard about the
idea of glasses that actually have the closed caption
inside. No one would necessarily even know that
they were using captions.

John, and other deaf individuals like him, do not necessarily
want to have to let other individuals know that they are hearing impaired. With sophisticated electronic enabling devices,
they can simply get on with their lives.

The expense of sophisticated equipment is a barrier for
John. As he explains:

A portable TDD costs $400. I don't have one, but I
will some day. It takes time to accumulate the
money for it. I need an alarm for my bed—there
are many things I need....Money is a real problem.
The only thing the government does is supply
TDDs for people, and if you move out of the state
you have to give it back....It's almost a full-time job
to try and find out who can help you and give you
the resources.

John has considered having a cochlear implant, but is
afraid of complications from the surgery that could result in
his face becoming partially paralyzed. He feels that the
cochlear implant is probably a good idea for young children,
but not necessarily for older individuals such as himself.
Technology such as the TDD, therefore, is of particular importance to him.

> At the community college, we have access to TDDs, but it's still not easy.... Right now we have to sign in and wait and wait and be patient. We need more computers that are accessible for deaf people. The college has been pretty insensitive to hearing impaired people. It's hard, but hopefully it will get better.

John emphasizes that computers that are set aside for deaf students at the community college need to include more specially designed tutoring devices and programs. He is constantly interested in finding out about new technologies and how they can help him:

> I try to find out about new technology....about new things that are invented. I learned about the TDD from a teacher I had in high school and I was amazed at what a difference it could make. I started talking on the phone all the time. I started to become proud of myself and more equal to other people. Before that I really felt that deaf people were less, and that they couldn't communicate. When I found that I could start leading a more normal life by communicating, I started feeling more proud about myself and more confident. And after I started to learn the system, I started to operate just like everybody else. People could learn how to call me back. It wasn't just with deaf people. I started reaching out to hearing people.

John sees important changes having occurred in the few years since he was in elementary school. According to him:

> When I was in elementary school, they didn't really have that much technology. Recently, I went to visit an elementary school here in Miami because I was curious to compare how it is now to when I was in school. I was shocked to find that elementary kids are now using computers and the computer is telling them in their speech therapy when they are making the correct sounds. So they are able to visually learn

to use their voices and that is so much of an improvement over what I had in therapy....It was so embarrassing, because I never knew if I was doing it right or wrong. And now I just wish I could go back.

John is an example of someone who is involved in the transition from old to new technologies. While he clearly benefits from TDD technology and systems for closed captioning for film and television, he feels he is too old to benefit from some of the newer technologies available for deaf individuals. This situation is a difficult one. While a cochlear implant may be a viable option for a younger individual, it seems to be very frightening for an adult like John, and therefore a difficult option to pursue. Working on his speech patterns may also be very difficult, since John feels it may be too late for him to start over again with his learning.

We are concerned that many aspects of adaptive technology could in fact benefit individuals like John and believe that special efforts must be made to connect these adults to the potential provided by technology.

RESEARCH

Research on the effect of technology on individuals with speech and hearing problems has yielded mixed results. A study by Laura Meyers found that when toddlers with Down's syndrome and cerebral palsy had control of speech output on a computer they spoke more themselves. School-aged children with Down's syndrome often use telegraphic one- to four-word utterances instead of complete sentences. Using a talking word processor these children have learned to speak and write in grammatical and multi-word sentences. Seeing the text on the screen combined with hearing the synthesized speech leads to improved spoken language skills. Non-speaking individuals with severe motor problems can communicate spontaneously using the computer and alternative input devices. Children who were previously thought to be incapable of achieving literacy have been able to write, and have even written books.[6]

Jeffrey Braden and Steven Shaw have put together a review of literature and meta-analysis of the literature describing computer applications with deaf children, which suggests that computer-assisted instruction is no better than alternative forms of instruction. Computers are neither panacea or poison, but may only be an expensive placebo.[7]

In a study of the vocabulary learning of eight severely handicapped toddlers, a computer-based approach was compared to a traditional intervention technique. Subjects made similar progress regardless of the intervention they received.[8]

Philip Prinz and Keith Nelson investigated the effects of microcomputer technology on writing and reading skills of thirty-two deaf children, three to eight years of age. Using an Apple computer with a large keyboard and interchangeable overlays, children were able to explore and interact with the computer. Results indicated that through this interactive approach children demonstrated improved writing, reading, and general communication skills.[9]

CONCLUSION

Adaptive technology can open new worlds for individuals with speech and hearing disabilities. Its use with the speech impaired, for example, can allow individuals who have suffered from a stroke or who have degenerative nerve or muscle diseases to speak and communicate through a synthesizer, when previously they could not speak at all. For the individual who is deaf or hearing impaired, the computer and its related technologies can make telecommunication possible, as well as provide access to sources of information and knowledge normally available only to those who can hear. Such technologies have the potential to not only make individuals with disabilities more productive, but to enrich their lives by providing them with the effective means to reach out and respond to people in the world around them.

6

ADAPTIVE TECHNOLOGY
AND THE
COGNITIVELY IMPAIRED

At the beginning of this book we discussed the role of the computer in augmenting human intellect. In this context, the computer is useful not only for enhancing and extending intellectual capabilities, but also in helping remediate and compensate for cognitive impairment and limitations. The most common types of cognitive impairment are learning disabilities and certain types of decreased general mental functioning, as in mental retardation.

The onset of a cognitive disability can occur at any time during an individual's life. Genetic abnormalities, prenatal conditions, and birth complications can result in cognitive deficits that manifest themselves from birth. Head trauma and other damage to the brain can happen as a result of accidents or disease processes. Strokes can occur in both the young and the old, but are more common in older individuals. Various forms of dementia, including Alzheimer's disease, usually occur later in life.

Since cognitively impaired individuals often have speech and language deficits, much of the technology developed to aid those with speech and language problems is also appropriate for these individuals.

LEARNING DISABILITIES

The most widely used definition of learning disabilities is the one incorporated in the Education for All Handicapped

Act, also known as Public Law 94–142. According to the law's definition:

> Specific learning disability means a disorder in one or more of the basic psychological processes involved in understanding or in using language spoken or written, which may manifest itself in an imperfect ability to listen, think, speak, write, spell, or do mathematical calculations. The term includes such conditions as perceptual handicaps, brain injury, minimal brain dysfunction, dyslexia, and developmental aphasia. The term does not include children who have learning problems which are primarily the result of visual, hearing or motor handicaps, of mental retardation, of emotional disturbance, or of environmental, cultural or economic disadvantage.[1]

The major concepts underlying this definition include that the individual (1) has a disorder in one or more of the basic psychological processes; (2) has difficulty in learning; (3) has problems that are not primarily due to other causes such as visual, hearing, or motor handicaps; and (4) has a severe discrepancy between his or her potential for learning and actual level of achievement.[2]

Students with learning disabilities comprise the single largest group of school children who have handicapping conditions. The population of individuals with learning disabilities includes those with attention deficit/hyperactivity problems. These individuals need extensive drill and practice due to problems in processing information. Game-like formats, structured content, and the immediate reinforcement provided by many computer programs work well for these individuals who often have short attention spans. Increased motivation and attention to rote learning tasks has been observed in students using computer-assisted instruction. For example, a study by MacArthur et. al. compared computer-assisted instruction with paper and pencil instruction as means of providing independent practice in spelling with fifth and sixth grade learning disabled students. The group using computers spent significantly more time engaged on task as well as scored higher on spelling achievement.[3]

Individuals with learning disabilities may have difficulty with sensory input, such as visual or auditory perception, or memory problems. For example, persons with auditory memory problems are helped by seeing visual representations of what they are hearing. Individuals with visual perception problems can learn by hearing spoken words along with what they are seeing. The computer is a particularly effective means of providing this type of multisensory learning. Also, for individuals with learning disabilities who are not yet able to read, the computer can read information aloud, so the individual's academic progress is not delayed while he or she is learning to read. The Council for Exceptional Children has recommended computer programs with voice output to provide students with learning disabilities with auditory feedback.[4]

Children with learning disabilities may also have social and emotional problems. The computer, used in small groups, can become a means to encourage sharing, cooperation, social interaction, and social learning. Working together on problem-solving software such as Broderbund's Where in the World is Carmen Santiago? or Sunburst's The Pond can help students address their social-communication problems.

Many children with learning disabilities have difficulty with paper and pencil tasks. These children have problems writing their ideas, and then are further frustrated by having to correct spelling mistakes and to rewrite several times. The computer, used with word processing software, enables children with illegible handwriting to produce legible print instead of their awkward script.

In general, children with learning disabilities tend to be fearful of making errors. Computer-based tools, such as word processors, outlining programs, and spelling and grammar checkers, help make the writing environment more manageable and appealing. Word processing programs make it easy to correct mistakes. The computer provides a tool that enables individuals with learning disabilities to revise and edit their work more easily. It bypasses the fine motor control needed to produce legible writing and it eliminates messy eraser smudges and the need to rewrite. Spelling and grammar-checking software, such as Write This Way (which was described in the previous chapter), is programmed to address the errors made by students with learning disabilities. These errors typically include run-on sentences, scrambled letters, inappropriate syntax, and mistakes in capitalization and punctuation. This software, which includes speech output so students can hear what they have written, is designed to help individuals with learning disabilities increase their ability to correct their own mistakes.

Co:Writer, available from Don Johnston, Incorporated, is an example of word prediction software that can help students with learning disabilities with their writing. This software, which works with a word processor, uses principles of artificial intelligence to predict the next word, thus reducing the number of keystrokes required. It provides grammatically correct word choices, correct spelling, and help with sentence construction.

Word prediction software works as follows: when a single letter is typed, up to ten words which begin with that letter are predicted. The writer then selects the desired word. The first word of the sentence is automatically capitalized. After the first word has been selected, the software predicts the next word choices using such grammar rules as subject-verb agreement, verb tense and usage, as well as word relationships, frequency, recency, and redundancy. It helps students with learning disabilities put words in the right order and helps them to organize their thoughts, and with grammar and spelling. Speech feedback and automatic scanning are some of the options provided by this software.

Research on using word processors to improve writing has revealed that students tend to make more revisions with word processors, but that these changes are typically only in spelling, punctuation, and text length. Skills in written expression are not improved through the use of word processing alone. However, students do learn to write better when word processing is incorporated into a program of systematic instruction in written expression. Numerous studies have confirmed that students become more confident and proud of their writing and they believe that their writing improves when they use a word processor.[5] Providing students with a laptop computer to use for all writing activities at home and at school, has been successful in helping students with learning disabilities.[6]

Computer software for individuals with learning disabilities needs to include simple directions (perhaps graphic or animated), suggested strategies for getting answers available on request, feedback that explains the reasons for mistakes, and suggestions for arriving at the correct responses. Learners should be able to easily access on-screen instructions and help functions. Computer software should also provide opportunities to try alternative answers, give consistent positive reinforcement, remove time constraints, and provide approximations that lead the user toward correct responses and answers. This software should be self-paced and non-threatening. It should inform students of the number of their correct responses, not their incorrect ones, and display helpful prompts. Software for children with learning disabilities should improve attention to task. It should also help them with the visual recognition of letters, shapes, numbers, and colors, as well as the sequencing of tasks and other learning skills such as organizing written material and developing vocabulary. Another important characteristic of software for students with learning disabilities is that it should include the capability to be easily controlled by teachers as well as by learners. Teachers should be able to modify content, criteria, feedback, cuing and prompts, repetition, and practice drills.

A great deal of software has become available in recent years that makes it possible for learning disabled and other individuals who are cognitively impaired to enhance and develop their cognitive functions. One such program is The Optimum Resource Reading Program developed by Optimum Resource Inc., which is a voice-interactive microcomputer system designed for children with learning disabilities. It uses natural-sounding digitized speech and voice recognition to talk and listen to students. Providing a series of interactive lessons based on current research about reading disabilities, The Optimum Resource Reading Program includes clear instructions and positive reinforcement for its users, monitors progress, and individualizes lessons.

Other software which is appropriate for individuals with learning disabilities is the Edmark Reading Program. This beginning reading program teaches users to recognize and comprehend 350 words. It incorporates all learning modalities, introduces new information in small steps, and provides multiple repetitions for reinforcement. The program includes spoken voice functions and can be used with a keyboard, joystick, or touch window.

The Reading Tutor developed by the Kurzweil Reading Machine Division of Xerox Imaging Systems is a computer-based software system that improves reading speed and comprehension through oral and written text material. It is recommended for individuals who have dyslexia and other learning disabilities, as well as for the rehabilitation of individuals who have had stroke or head injury. Because this system provides for the scanning of any printed text, it is able to produce reading materials appropriate to individual interests and abilities.

The computer, with appropriate instructional software, can help not only individuals with learning disabilities, but also other mildly handicapped persons, such as those who are developmentally delayed or emotionally disturbed. It can help them acquire the skills, processes, attitudes, and behaviors they need to meet the objectives of mainstream learning.

Catherine Garcia, an individual with learning disabilities, uses basic computer technology to help her function better.

CATHERINE GARCIA: A CASE STUDY OF ADAPTIVE TECHNOLOGY FOR AN INDIVIDUAL WITH LEARNING DISABILITIES

Catherine is in her early twenties and a student at Miami Dade Community College in Miami, Florida. She is working toward a degree in business administration with an emphasis on hotel management.

As Catherine describes her disability:

> It takes me a while to understand certain subjects—
> I can understand reading because that's my favorite
> subject. Others take me a little bit longer time....
> History—dates, trying to remember dates, names,
> places—I don't have a really good memory....I can
> remember certain dates, I can't remember certain
> things. I remember streets, places, driving, but not
> history books.

For Catherine, mathematics is a difficult subject because of the formulas and the way teachers explain the material. She also has some trouble with subjects like English, but not as much. Catherine has been fortunate in that her mother has always helped her with her work.

> My mom helps me a lot—when I was small she put me in the best schools with special programs. I was treated differently from the kids but it helped me get into the school system. Without it I think I would have dropped out of school a long time ago.

Catherine was first identified as having learning disabilities when she was in elementary school. She was given special tests and her disabilities were identified. She had particular difficulties with eye-hand coordination and speech. School was often a difficult place for her. One of her elementary school teachers, for example, threw her out of class for being lazy because she could not understand what was being taught. As Catherine recalls:

> They didn't know what to do with handicapped students. Unless you were retarded, or with Down's syndrome....They put me in regular classes. My mother put me in Teachers College (Columbia University) in New York for Speech....There was a two-way mirror. Students were recording us, watching us....My speech teacher would help me with sounds and cards. They found out I had dyslexia. I would see letters backwards. I still do that sometimes.

In junior high school Catherine was teased about her disabilities. As a result, she often got into fights and arguments. Throughout high school she also went to night school in order to try to keep up academically. It was clear that her special needs were not being adequately met. There was no special equipment for her and only limited opportunities for special tutoring.

Graduating from high school was, according to her, the "biggest thrill" of her life. On completing high school she began course work at a community college in the New York area and then moved with her family to Miami. In New York, she found herself largely on her own in her studies, although she was assigned a special education counselor.

> With my permission he would go to my professors and tell them I had a learning disability so when I had a test I would be allowed more time. Test time was one thing (over which) I would panic. I would freeze. I could not remember the information—I would freeze.

While at the community college in New York Catherine began to use computers. "I took a class to learn how to do it. They were very helpful, much faster than a typewriter. We had a certain program, you could look up spelling words, dictionary words." Although there were special computer programs available from the college for doing work in subject areas such as mathematics, it was not clear to Catherine how she could get access to them. She recalls that in order to use the programs she would have to find an empty classroom with a computer in it.

For a student like Catherine, getting ready access to a computer posed a considerable problem. Eventually her sister got a computer for her own work and let Catherine use it.

> I would do my papers, if I had an English paper to do I would do it on her computer which was the best thing...because it helped me with spelling and dictionary meanings. And it was quicker. You put in the information and zip.

Throughout her interview, it was evident that even basic computer programs such as a word processing and spell checking systems made an important difference to Catherine in being able to keep up with her academic work. Despite this fact, it was clear from her description of her experience that she did not have access to a computer.

If, as we have argued earlier, the computer is a tool for augmenting one's thinking, then not having computer support on a regular ongoing basis is like not having a prosthetic arm or leg available for an amputee. The computer is an absolutely essential tool for someone like Catherine, and her access to the machine cannot be on an intermittent basis. It should not be assumed that someone like her will have the necessary personal or financial resources to gain access to appropriate technology. Instead, such resources must be integrated into her educational program.

In light of the moderate cost of portable computers and the ready availability of a variety of useful software, there is little or no excuse for failing to provide individuals like Catherine with a reasonable computer environment in which to work. When asked in her interview whether someone like herself could get assistance in getting her own computer, Catherine indicated that this was only possible if you had a profoundly handicapping condition. "I believe you really have to have special handicap problems...like being stuck in a wheelchair, or being mentally retarded or stuff like that." For individuals like Catherine, not having a computer available on a regular basis puts her at an unnecessary disadvantage.

MENTAL RETARDATION

According to the definition provided by the American Association on Mental Retardation (AAMR):

> Mentally retarded refers to significantly subaverage general intellectual functioning resulting in or associated with deficits in adaptive behavior, and manifested during the developmental period.[7]

Although this description has been adopted by the AAMR, there is still considerable controversy over the definition and characteristics of mental retardation. Another area of controversy is over the classification of mentally retardation by type or severity. One means of classifying is according to cause or etiology, which is helpful to the medical profession. Another way of classifying is in terms of severity, as measured by intelligence test scores, which is more useful to educators. The AAMR defines the following categories of mental retardation: (1) Mild, also referred to as educable mentally retarded (EMR), which includes individuals with intelligence test scores between 50 and 75; (2) Moderate, also referred to as trainable mentally retarded (TMR), which includes scores of approximately 35 to 50; (3) Severe, which includes those individuals with scores of approximately 20 to 35; and (4) Profound, which is below 20.[8] Many of the individuals in the severe and profound categories also have other handicapping conditions.[9]

Individuals who are mentally retarded demonstrate less-than-average capabilities across many functions as opposed to individuals with learning disabilities who have problems with only affected areas of intellectual functioning. The computer can be an appropriate learning tool for individuals who are retarded because it is "patient." Teachers tend to provide an answer after a certain amount of time has passed, but the computer can be programmed to wait for even the slowest individual to respond. Computer programs can provide feedback that is immediate as well as interesting through the use of graphics and sound. The computer can be programmed to accept as many mistakes as necessary without giving negative responses. Another advantage of the computer is that it can be programmed to present information in very small units. Using the computer also provides the user with a sense of cause and effect and a means of control.

Speech output is important in programs for individuals who are cognitively challenged because they often have limited competence in reading. Programs that include spoken directions and responses are very helpful to these individuals.

Individuals with severe cognitive delays or limitations often have difficulty using a standard keyboard. Adaptations such as joysticks, touchscreens, or expanded keyboards, along with simplified commands, can help make computers more accessible for these individuals. Voice recognition input systems are helpful for individuals who cannot remember long or complicated keystrokes. Instead they can use simple spoken commands.

For individuals with cognitive delays, simple cause and effect programs are appropriate. Public domain and other programs in which activating a switch or other input device results in a picture, sound and/or music, help develop the concept of cause and effect. Once an individual has mastered how to activate an input device and create some type of sound or visual output, he or she can move into the next level of very simple programs involving choices.

Much of the software that has been developed for the general population can be used by individuals who are learning disabled and cognitively challenged. Many of the programs for young children are appropriate for cognitively challenged individuals, particularly those programs that focus on attention to a task, visual discrimination, visual and auditory memory, sequencing, and following directions. Memory and problem solving skills can also be addressed by computer software.

The computer can also be helpful for individuals with brain injury due to strokes or head trauma. Computer programs can be used to train areas of the brain that were not damaged to take over functions that have been impaired. IBM, for example, has a program called *THINKable*, which is designed to sharpen the minds of people suffering from cognitive disability as a result of head injuries, neurological disorders, or substance abuse. *THINKable* breaks cognitive functions into memory, attention, discrimination, and sequencing, and tests each of these functions at four different levels. Users respond to tasks using a touch screen. Feedback on responses is given with speech output. This program provides more accurate and customized diagnosis of cognitive functioning than can be typically provided by more conventional forms of therapy.

Adaptive Technology and Individuals Who Are Cognitively Impaired: An Interview With Carol Farrell

Mike Morgan, whose case study was included in the previous chapter, is an example of a student who is cognitively impaired and effectively using adaptive technology. In Mike's case, not only was he disabled cognitively, but he also had severe physical and speech impairments. Interviewing individuals with severe cognitive limitations is obviously difficult, if not impossible. As a result, we have decided in this final research chapter to deviate from our case study model of interviewing individuals who are taking advantage of adaptive technology, and instead interview Carol Farrell, a professional who is actively involved in using adaptive technology with cognitively impaired students.

Carol is a speech pathologist at the Seagull Center for Physically Impaired and Autistic Students, a public school center funded by the Broward County, Florida, schools. Carol explains that the children with whom she works are:

> ...in the educable mentally handicapped range. It is difficult to get an accurate measure of their potential to learn. These students are ages five to twenty-two. Most of them are non-speaking or speech impaired. Some are eligible for this center as physically handicapped and are not yet categorized as mentally handicapped. In middle and secondary school, students must be designated as educable or trainable in order to earn a diploma. That is when they are tested to determine eligibility for educable mentally handicapped or trainable mentally handicapped categories.
>
> Since these students can't speak or write, it is difficult for them to participate in academic tasks. However, they can use communication devices such as the Touch Talker, Light Talker, and Real Voice systems to help them work on assignments. They can use a switch, pointer, or whatever input method they are capable of using, with the communication device, which can then be hooked to a printer, creating a written product. Thus the student can input answers or responses and the teacher is able to check the display or printout of what the student has done. Students are learning because they are doing it themselves. They are choosing letters, putting letters together and making choices.
>
> For example, in the intermediate grades, students can use the same workbooks and textbooks as the rest of the class. They can use their communication device to practice spelling words or find the spelling words in a sentence. In upper grades students can use the Light Talker to copy sentences using spelling words and print them out. Most of these students do not have the literacy skills to actually compose original sentences using the spelling words.

Carol explains that each of the classrooms at the Center has an Apple IIGS and a Macintosh computer and a variety of input devices including switches, expanded and miniaturized keyboards, and touch sensitive screens.

Carol describes her students using these different systems:

> One student Fred, who is nineteen years of age, came to the Seagull Center having had no confidence in himself, and with severe cognitive limitations. He now uses Real Voice for communication and for academic tasks, such as copying words, and is able to ask for a drink of water or to use the bathroom....He also uses his communication device to ask questions of people who come into his classroom.
>
> Laura, who is classified as trainable mentally handicapped, is both outgoing and social. She started at the Center about three years ago. She is twenty years old and can attend the program in Broward County until she is twenty-one. She uses Real Voice with a Min Key overlay. She is able to access the system using a switch activated by her right foot, which is the only controllable movement she has. Laura has limited literacy skills, but is able to do logical letter coding. She uses the Real Voice device into which routines for certain kinds of conversation have been programmed. Recently, for example, she was trying to communicate where she went out to eat dinner. She spelled "World of Italy." The teacher finally figured out she meant "The Olive Garden." Using the Real Voice and Min Key systems, the quantity and quality of her interactions has significantly increased.
>
> · A major problem for both Fred and Laura is that the communication devices they use belong to the school, and are not taken home with them. Use of these devices produces significant gains. But then it is too much trouble to move the devices around from one classroom to the other and set them up, so they aren't used all the time. The teacher will often take the time to set them up for academic tasks, but not just for communication. If the students owned

the devices and were able to attach them to their wheel chairs, they could use the devices all the time.

On the other hand, some of the students at the Center have never had a communication device. Students are introduced to communication devices and then we work towards each student having his/her own. Typically, the speech pathologist or another school-related professional pursues funding for these devices. A few parents have insurance.

Devices become obsolete quickly. In three or four years, the individual needs a new one. When combined with other expenses like medical expenses and wheel chairs, these communication devices become a low priority for parents with limited financial resources. For example a Liberator and switch mounting cost about nine thousand dollars.

Carol explains that purchasing new technology is simply not enough for cognitively limited students, but getting it to function effectively for them is the key. As she explains:

A commonly held belief is that if only the money were available, technology would really help these individuals. But the money is only the beginning. Getting new technology, getting it set up and running fast isn't enough, since then it often doesn't work or do what it was expected to do and negative attitudes are created.

A match between the technology and the individual's needs is very important. It is better to wait until you can get the appropriate device. Otherwise it is said, "We tried technology and it didn't work." The least expensive is not always the best.

Carol explains that the use of computers for the cognitively limited student and the regular student is in many respects very similar.

The computer offers mentally handicapped individuals what it offers other students. It is more interesting and motivating. It enables them to work independently. It provides different levels which allow for individualization. A problem with using the computer for the cognitively impaired is finding the right software. For trainable mentally handicapped individuals the need is to find software with the skill they need to work on at their level. Much of the software is written at a level that is too difficult for them.

TECHNOLOGY ACROSS THE LIFE SPAN

There are four major goals of adaptive technology use that apply to all ages: (1) communication (spoken and written language), (2) cognitive stimulation and development, (3) recreation, leisure, and play (includes music, art, games) and (4) environmental control. These four areas of competence are important to individuals at all age levels.

Technology can play an important role throughout the lives of individuals with special needs, including the very young. It can help expand a young child's potential to interact, learn, and develop.

The primary aim of using technology with young children with disabilities is to allow these children access to the assistive technology that will be most appropriate to their needs and to provide for maximum participation in social and educational environments. Technology can help reach the goal of full participation and inclusion of children of all abilities.

A major purpose of early education is to foster competence in young children; not only intellectual competence, but competence relating to the physical, emotional, social, and creative self. One of the major benefits of technology for young children with disabilities is that it can help them develop a sense of competence. The desire for competence is one of the basic motivators of human behavior.[10] Humans have an inherent drive for mastery and competence. Helplessness is the opposite of competence. A number of studies have demonstrated that feelings of helplessness result when children find that their personal effort has little impact on how things turn out.[11] When they experience consistent failure, some children conclude that nothing they do makes any difference, therefore they just stop trying. Young children with disabilities often learn helplessness because they cannot use traditional methods to impact their environment. Adaptive technology provides a way for them to learn cause and effect—to learn that they can have an effect and they can make something happen. Replacing learned helplessness with a feeling of competence helps children see themselves in control, at least to some degree, of what happens to them. They begin to feel good about themselves and have a sense that they will be able to manage most situations and will be able to cope with whatever they encounter.

Technology can help give young children with disabilities the ability to communicate; being able to communicate is part of having a sense of control and is of great importance to children with special needs. Children need to be able to express themselves, and feel that they are heard and accepted.

The importance of play as a way for young children to learn is recognized by early childhood educators. Battery-operated toys and switches can be tools for developing play skills with objects and with peers. For children who are either chronologically or developmentally very young, using a switch to control a battery-operated adapted toy is an appropriate introduction to technology. Children learn that when they activate a switch something happens. This helps children develop the concepts of cause and effect, means/end causality, intentional behavior and making choices.

After children have a variety of experiences with toys and switches, they are better prepared to have successful interactions with the computer. The computer can be adapted for young children in several ways including the use of switch input, Unicorn Keyboard, PowerPad, Muppet Learning Keys, TouchWindow and speech output.

The Unicorn Keyboard provides children who could not use a standard keyboard access to a computer. The Unicorn Keyboard, the PowerPad, and the TouchWindow can all be customized for individual children in several ways. For example, pictures of members of a child's family can be placed on blank overlays. These areas can then be programmed so that when a particular area of an overlay is pressed, the name of the family

member is spoken by a speech synthesizer. An overlay may
have pictures from different nursery rhymes. Pressing a picture
of a character from one of the nursery rhymes would result in
hearing that particular rhyme. The Unicorn Keyboard can be
made to look more and more like a regular keyboard, thus per-
mitting children to enter the mainstream. The TouchWindow is
a particularly appropriate input device for young children because they don't have to look from the keyboard to the monitor.
They can focus on the monitor for both input and output.

The value of young children's experiences with technology
is determined in large part by the software. A range of developmentally appropriate software is becoming available for young
children—programs that are animated, oriented toward problem solving, and challenging enough to hold their interest.
Generally the best software is that which fosters interaction
and is open-ended.

Adaptive Technology and Young Children With Disabilities: An Interview With Nina Kaspar

How adaptive technology can be incorporated into the
work and teaching of preschool educators can be seen in the
case of Nina Kasper, a preschool varying exceptionalities
teacher at Colonial Drive Elementary School in Miami,
Florida. Nina has been teaching for about eight years. An ener-
getic and upbeat individual in her life and teaching, she is a
convert to using computers with students in her class. As she
explained to us:

> Computers and technology are the way to go in spe-
> cial education in general. And since we're looking at
> special education, you can't just be short-sighted.
> You have to look at the whole picture. It is crucial to
> start at three years of age or even sooner. And that
> doesn't necessarily always mean computers, per se.
> There are a lot of prerequisite things that go into it
> for kids: cause and effect, choice making, attention
> things, and visual things. It depends on the child
> and his exceptionality, of course.
>
> In my classroom, which is for individuals
> with varying exceptionalities, there are some pretty

involved kids. At the same site we also have a main-streamed group with normally developing kids. So we've been able to use our computers in many different ways...for individual children to meet their needs as well as a nice opportunity for mainstreaming.

We have two computers that we are using right now in addition to other equipment. We have a Macintosh LC with all the peripherals and then I have an old Apple IIGS. One of the problems we have in the schools is that we have to lock down computers and other expensive equipment and that doesn't give you the flexibility you sometimes need with computers. The GS isn't locked down, so I am able to put it on the floor, put it on kids' trays and do a lot more with it, although it is not as sophisticated as the Macintosh. For that reason we keep a lot of the cause and effect, public domain, and switch access software on the Apple IIGS and some of the more sophisticated software like Kid Pix on the Macintosh. But it's really interesting because we have children functioning from about six months to normally developing kids. And you would think that kids would pick software according to their developmental level. But it's not always true. All of the children really enjoy the cause and effect stuff and they all achieve success using it. We really keep a lot of our stuff open ended and success oriented. And the kids have success, especially the kids with lower cognitive abilities or lower physical abilities.

The children in my class are developmentally from six months to two and a half years, although the chronological age of the children is three to five years. Most of the children have cerebral palsy, either totally spastic quadriplegic or some part of their body affected. Barely any of my children are verbal (verbal meaning communicative). There are some verbalizations, but most communication is through other means such as gesture or guessing or pointing. That's why I'm using a lot of adaptive technology besides computers with a lot of the kids.

Adaptive technology, according to Nina, is not without its problems. Equipment becomes outdated, software does not do everything it needs to do, and things break. As Nina explained:

> A major frustration in using computers is when they break down either because the children misuse them or because of something that happened in the computer. There is usually only one person at the site who knows much about computers so when something breaks down that person has to try to fix it. It would help teachers of young children if computers were designed so that the disk drive was out of the way or covered....Dependability, being sturdy, and accessibility are key things in designing the computer.

For Nina, the major contribution of adaptive technology is the success it provides her students:

> Success. Success and motivation. I've had kids with cerebral palsy, kids with Down's syndrome, kids with autism, kids with almost any exceptionality. And for almost any kid I can find something on the computer that will make them happy. And I can't name too many other pieces of equipment or toys or materials that I can get that many kids to be interested in.

The computer is as effective as it is, according to Nina, because of its flexibility and open-endedness.

> If it is open-ended, it's automatic reinforcement. If it's the right program, you touch something and something happens. For a lot of these kids this doesn't happen. Even with simple toys, they can't make them do what they are supposed to do, or maybe they don't even know what they are supposed to do. But you put a touch window on the computer with a little cause and effect program, and you touch it and something happens. It's the same as a switch toy. You touch the switch and the toy moves. And the

cause and effect foundation is everything. Until a kid has that, you can't move him forward.

For Nina, computers are particularly valuable because they can be reprogrammed and adapted to the specific needs of students:

> Communication is my thing. At the preschool level we usually don't buy each child a communication device because we don't know yet exactly what each one will need. Some of them may have verbal language eventually. But the computer enables the teacher to experiment with what some of the options are without having to have individual equipment for everybody.

Another benefit Nina saw in using computers with her children was the way in which they contributed to motor development.

> The computer is really good for motor skills. For fine motor skills we write into the children's Individual Education Plan (IEP) such goals as being able to put the right amount of pressure on the touch window, isolating fingers on the keyboard or using two hands. Gross motor skills include pulling self to a stand in order to use the computer, good head control, and good sitting. The computer is written into IEPs for both fine and gross motor control.

> Nina believes that enabling the child to control his or her environment empowers both the student and the teacher.

> The computer empowers both my students and me as a teacher. It gives me a lot of options of things I can do. I can use it for socialization. We set up one of our computers with a bench in front of it instead of chairs so it forces children to sit next to each other. And usually there is a higher functioning kid and a lower functioning kid.
> The computer offers the teacher many options and I can have control if it's the right piece of soft-

ware, and many of the things I can program myself.
I can reinforce things I am doing in the classroom. It
gives me flexibility. Teachers love that. I love some of
the simple public domain touch window programs. I
can put the kids' pictures in there and things that are
meaningful for the kids in their environment, in
their home or in the classroom. You can't do that
with store-bought materials. This software can be
personalized to fit their needs and to fit my needs.

For Nina, the use of adaptive technology fosters the idea
of inclusion. As she explains:

We share an open space with a class of twenty children, which includes normally developing children,
where the computer is set up. The children just pop
in and out of the computer area at all times. There's
always a group of kids around the computer. The
special needs children often actively participate or
actively watch. There's always a different mix of
children at the computer. We really use the computer as a social place. We keep the GS on the floor
which is mostly for the children who need adaptive
positioning. But everyone just comes; kids from
both classes. Even when it's basic cause and effect
software, the four- and five-year-olds are interested
and hitting the switch to produce the smiley face.
    One of our most severely involved students is
just learning to hit the switch to make something
happen. Generally, some other kid comes along
while she is at the computer and hits the switch. It
is just so tempting even for the normally developing children to hit the switch to see what happens.
And then she comes alive. It is very amazing to see
what happens; to see how they interact. A severely
involved child with a switch toy soon draws a
crowd of five children who are interested in working the switch to see what happens. There is defin-
itely social interaction.
    Besides social interaction, we use computers
for communication; of course it encourages inclusion

that way too. It allows them to participate in activities where they might not be able to if it's language dependent.

The elderly are the fastest growing segment of the population. Many senior adults are experiencing decreased cognitive functioning, limited physical ability, or the combination of both mental and physical disabilities as a result of stroke or some other debilitating condition. Advances in medicine have helped provide a longer life span for these individuals. Now they need to be helped to live with dignity and to enjoy an acceptable quality of life. Technology has the potential to provide this better quality of life for senior adults.

Some of the problems faced by older individuals include communication difficulties; cognitive problems such as confusion, disorientation, and memory loss; decreased physical ability; and lack of motivation and interest. These senior adults may find that they are no longer able to meet basic self-care needs or to move independently within the environment. Young children with similar problems would probably be in some type of school setting where they would have an educational plan along with a support team to implement that plan. Senior adults, however, are likely to be in an extended care facility where decisions about care and treatment would be made by physicians, family, and any others who might make up the individual's treatment team. Both children and older adults can benefit from technology. The question is, will older individuals be given the same opportunity to benefit from technology as young people are given? Will older persons with multiple impairments be relegated to custodial care or will technology be used to improve their independent functioning?

Low technology devices are currently being used to help older adults function independently. Adaptations such as feeding devices, shower chairs, and enlarged print are commonly used by these individuals and are relatively inexpensive. But with the elderly being the fastest growing segment of the population, more resources will be needed to provide access to additional technology that could provide a means to communicate, some control over the environment, and the pleasure of interaction and cognitive stimulation.

Technology can be used to increase the involvement and interaction of older individuals whose ability to function is limited physically or cognitively. The use of battery-operated games, single switch computer programs, and augmentative communication can be included as part of their therapy and activity programs. Games can motivate purposeful action and can rekindle interest and even excitement, enabling individuals to change from passive observers to active participants. Switch-operated tape recorders can provide access to music or tape recordings made by loved ones.

Cognitive rehabilitation can be facilitated by using single switch and public domain software to reestablish an understanding of cause and effect and a sense of control. By activating a switch, a picture or music is produced. Most of the available software is for children; software more appropriate for older adults would be helpful.

Technology can also be used to give these senior adults a sense of empowerment and control, which can increase independence. Switch usage may be among the individual's most purposeful activity. Using a single switch to turn on a radio or to assist in communication can provide an increased sense of control and decrease the sense of helplessness that comes with lack of ability to affect the environment. Word processing software can assist seniors in writing for pleasure or for communication. They can use software to create word searches or crossword puzzles, which can be shared. Speech evaluation systems, such as IBM's *SpeechViewer* that was described in chapter 5, could help in the process of reteaching older individuals to speak.

Technology can be a bridge between the generations and help facilitate interactions between senior adults and family members. Children are using computers and are comfortable with them. If senior adults have computers, they can use switches or other adapted input devices to play games and have fun with their grandchildren or other family members.

CONCLUSION

In this chapter we have provided an overview of how adaptive technology can maximize the function of individuals who are cognitively impaired. In this context, the idea of the computer as a means of augmenting intellect or cognition is critical. For the student who is learning disabled, the computer can provide the potential to function normally when this otherwise would not be possible. For the person who is severely or profoundly retarded, the computer becomes an essential means by which to reach out to, communicate, and interact with the world.

As is the case with persons with physical disabilities, the use of adaptive technology has the potential to break down major barriers for individuals who are cognitively limited— barriers that would otherwise be almost impossible to overcome. In doing so, adaptive technology not only provides remediation for the cognitively impaired, but can also compensate for limitations resulting from disabilities, in areas such as vision, speech, and hearing and the physical domain.

7

HYPERMEDIA AND INDIVIDUALS WITH SPECIAL NEEDS

This work outlines a range of hardware and software that can be used to help individuals with varying needs. Almost all of these technologies came into widespread use in the late 1970s and throughout the 1980s. Many of these innovations are extremely valuable and will continue to be used in years to come. One of the most interesting new developments in hardware and software is the introduction and use of hypertext and hypermedia.

We believe that hypertext and hypermedia will see an increase in adaptive technology applications in the future. This chapter defines hypertext and hypermedia, describes their general use in education, and provides ideas about how hypertext and hypermedia can be used by those with special needs.

DEFINING HYPERTEXT AND HYPERMEDIA

Ted Nelson, a pioneer in the field of hypertext and hypermedia, defines hypertext as *"non-sequential writing—text that allows choice to the reader, best read as an interactive screen."*[1] Most simply understood, this represents "a series of text chunks connected by links which offers the reader different pathways."[2] Jeff Conklin describes hypertext as "direct machine-supported references from one textual chunk to another." As he explains:

The concept of hypertext is quite simple: Windows
on the screen are associated with objects in a database and links are provided between these objects,
both graphically (as labelled) and in the database
(as pointers).[3]

Hypermedia is essentially hypertext that is not just textually
based, but that includes other attributes such as line art, photographs, animation, and sound. Throughout the rest of this
chapter, we will use the term hypermedia instead of hypertext—assuming that it includes or subsumes the latter.

Hypermedia can also be defined as the ability to link any
place in a text with any other place in the same or different
texts. Imagine for a moment a button included on the page of
a book which, when pressed, would take you to another page
in the book, or to another book, or to a special library. Imagine
a button that would take you to a recording, or a film, or a
photograph that is related to the text.

The use of hypermedia is important in the field of adaptive
technology in that it makes it possible for people with special
needs to not only have access to data, but also to expand the
use of their senses in ways that would not otherwise be possible. A simple example of how a hypermedia system could be
used by a physically challenged individual can be seen in the
following case.

Read the following sentence:

Hypermedia is an esoteric concept.

Suppose that you were paralyzed and were reading this
sentence in a book that had been placed in front of you.
Perhaps you were beginning to understand the meaning of the
word hypermedia, but had no idea of what was meant by the
word esoteric. You would probably want to look up the word
in a dictionary, but your physical condition would make that
impossible. Your only solution would be to call someone to
look up the word for you.

If you are reading the same sentence on a computer that
is using a hypermedia system, you could use an adaptive input
device—a switch or eyegaze system for example—which would
allow you to highlight the word esoteric and call its definition
up as a hypermedia window on your computer screen. The
window could then be activated so that the computer would

pronounce the word, read aloud its definition, and even provide a practical example of its use. Once you had the definition you needed, you could return to the original text.

The above example barely touches all the potential uses of hypermedia in the field of adaptive technology. The following pages will provide a series of examples of how hypermedia can uniquely meet the needs of individuals with disabilities. In particular, we will outline the potential applications and uses of hypermedia for each of the areas of disabilities we have described in previous chapters. These include: (1) Hypermedia and the Physically Impaired, (2) Hypermedia and the Visually Impaired, (3) Hypermedia and the Hearing Impaired, and (4) Hypermedia and the Cognitively Impaired.

HYPERMEDIA AND THE
PHYSICALLY IMPAIRED

At the beginning of this book we described how Richard Ruopp, the former president of Bank Street College in New York City, presented a speech to a large audience using a speech synthesizer in conjunction with a word processing program. Using a hypermedia presentation system, Ruopp could have also added special sound effects and graphics, or even included music, video clips, photographs and animation. Portions of speeches made by others, and segments of texts from various authors could all have been included. At first these might appear to be simply frills and add-ons, but think of how important they would be if Ruopp needed to explain something in more detail. For example, it is highly likely that he could have anticipated questions that might have been asked of him concerning different parts of his speech. At key points in his presentation, Ruopp could have embedded hypermedia buttons linked to detailed drawings, topical outlines, and even animations. Perhaps, Ruopp might have wanted to draw a diagram or sketch something to illustrate a point in his lecture. He could have prepared this using a graphics program and an adaptive input device prior to his speech, and then activated it as part of his hypermedia presentation.

Hypermedia systems can be used in other ways by physically challenged individuals. One useful application is to provide individuals with simulations of activities in which they could not otherwise participate. Thus a wheelchair-bound individual, who would be unable to go through the back streets of a medieval town such as Florence, Italy, because of its steps and cobbled streets, could do so in a hypermedia simulation. Similar hypermedia simulations could be undertaken by physically challenged individuals interested in touring a museum.

In fact, just such a hypermedia model called The *CyberSpace Museum* has been proposed by one of the authors of this work, Eugene F. Provenzo, Jr., and his colleague Marjorie Montague. Using the Smithsonian's National Museum of American Art as the test site, the proposed model could be adapted for use in other art museums, or in historical and scientific museums. It could be developed using Macintosh's *Hypercard* system, or MS-DOS based hypermedia systems such as *Toolbook*, *Linkway*, or *Director*.

The *CyberSpace Museum* would offer the user an array of interactive experiences by taking him or her on an electronic tour of the galleries and collections of the Smithsonian's National Museum of American Art. The program would allow the user to tour the museum in a realistic physical simulation. Using the system, "visitors" to the *CyberSpace Museum* would be able to walk from art object to art object, examine each in detail, as well as call up historical background on the artists and their works, and, using an artificial intelligence system that could answer yes/no questions, have "conversations" with museum staff. In addition, users would be introduced to techniques and methods used by various artists whose work was included in the museum's collections, and would be given the opportunity to create their own work in both "real" space and the computer's electronic or "cyber" space. Users would be able to control and manipulate objects and create and appreciate their own art in ways that would not otherwise be possible. Collage materials, for example, and the tools necessary to manipulate them would be available in electronic files and would be controlled through various input devices.

Other features of the program could include a personalized digital art gallery that would allow the user to display his or her own work, as well as to put together collections of favorite art works, not just from the National Museum of American Art but from other art museums as well.

Hypermedia technology of this type could increase the user's (1) knowledge of the arts, (2) interest in the arts, (3) creative expression, (4) knowledge of computers, and (5) self-efficacy. Hypermedia systems like the *Cyberspace Museum* would enable users to become more independent in their learning and increase their opportunities for appreciating and creating art for themselves. Essentially, hypermedia technology opens a whole new universe of creative experiences to the individual with disabilities.

HYPERMEDIA AND THE
VISUALLY IMPAIRED

For a visually impaired individual, a hypermedia system like the *CyberSpace Museum*, could provide alternative ways of experiencing the works included in a museum's collection. For those with limited vision, hypermedia buttons in the system could provide magnification functions. Thus text, or possibly a painting or some other work of art, could be magnified, so that the user could more easily see and appreciate objects in which he or she is interested.

Using devices like the OPTACON, the user could have a map of the museum translated into a tactual interface. Thus an individual could feel where rooms and galleries were located, as well as get an overall sense of the layout and design of the museum. The same device could also be used to translate text included on the system into braille or raised letters.

Probably the most important and practical use of the system would be its capability to read aloud to the user text that appears on the system's computer screen. Thus, in the model we are presenting, detailed descriptions of paintings and other works of art, background on artists, and similar information become available to the user.

As in the case of the paralyzed individual described earlier in this chapter, using an adaptive input device such as a screen reading program and a braille keyboard, the user could highlight words that he or she did not understand and have the definitions called up as hypermedia windows on the screen. Then, as with the physically challenged user, the window could be activated so that the system "reads" the word and its definition aloud.

One of the advantages of a well-designed hypermedia system is that it can provide virtually infinite layers of material behind a particular text or set of images. For a visually impaired or physically challenged individual, this means that sources such as encyclopedias can be more easily accessed than they can in their traditional print format. As systems become more sophisticated and we have major libraries of information available on CD-ROMs in hypermedia formats, the access of visually impaired and physically challenged individuals to major sources of data will increase.

HYPERMEDIA AND THE HEARING IMPAIRED

For a hearing impaired individual, a hypermedia system like the *CyberSpace Museum* could be particularly valuable. Able to see the art on the computer, a hearing impaired individual could use hypermedia buttons to access the presentation of text in American Sign Language, as well as animations to help understand concepts with which he has not had any experience. It would also be possible using a hypermedia system to have a waveform dictionary available for virtually every word a user might come across. A deaf individual trying to learn spoken English could call up a waveform pattern for a word anytime it appeared on the screen. Imagine for a moment a graduate student who is deaf wanting to make a presentation about surrealist artists of the 1920s and the work of the Dadaists. Words such as *surrealist* and *Dadaist* could be accessed and their pronunciation practiced and worked on before the presentation.

Other uses of hypermedia for the hearing impaired include closed captioned programming, which can be used in the context of CD-ROM, videodisc, or videotape. By providing a closed caption option, the system enables the user to either view a program with sound or with closed captioning. As a result, the hearing disabled individual gains access to a whole universe of information. The same system can be used by individuals with or without special needs.

Hearing impaired students must get information about the world around them through their eyes rather than their ears. Visual references to concepts and facts are extremely important for them. Hypermedia systems can provide vast visual data banks to support written material for hearing impaired users. These visual data bases can include still pictures, cartoons, animations, and motion pictures.

HYPERMEDIA AND THE COGNITIVELY IMPAIRED

In the case of the *CyberSpace Museum* a number of different hypermedia functions can be employed to support cognitively impaired individuals. Perhaps the most obvious function is to have text read aloud. Thus individuals with reading problems can have access to information. Likewise, dictionary support systems can be made readily available.

In addition, material can be presented according to the cognitive level of the individual. Thus in the *CyberSpace Museum* it would be possible to access a very simple tour of the museum—one intended for individuals with limited cognitive ability, or a more advanced level for individuals who can process information more easily.

Using digitizing devices, users can be included as part of the system on which they are working. For example, a photograph of a child can be scanned-in and incorporated into the program. Imagine a cognitively disabled child going through an art gallery or a photographic gallery and suddenly seeing his or her own picture included on the wall.

Going beyond the model of the *CyberSpace Museum*, imagine taking cognitively disabled students on a field trip, videotaping or photographing them, and then incorporating their images into a hypermedia story that they could write themselves and use as reading material.

CONCLUSION

This chapter suggests how hypermedia systems can be used as an enabling technology for the physically, visually, and hearing impaired and for cognitively challenged individuals. It is brief, since hypermedia is an emerging technology whose possibilities and uses for the challenged individual are just beginning to be explored.

In a certain sense, hypermedia systems naturally cross boundaries that are created by different abilities. One of the most important aspects of hypermedia as an enabling technology is the fact that a single system can be adapted to serve the needs of individuals with varying abilities. Thus in the case of a program like the *CyberSpace Museum*, a read-aloud function for text can assist individuals who are visually impaired or who have problems processing text materials, or those who just want to listen rather than read.

We believe that the real significance and excitement of hypermedia as an enabling technology is how it fosters the notion of inclusion for all individuals. A model such as the *CyberSpace Museum* is exciting because it can be used by virtually anyone—with or without disabilities. Thus ideas, information, and experiences can be shared across different groups, providing the foundations for a more inclusive and democratic culture.

In conclusion, hypertext and hypermedia are powerful tools for creating enabling technologies, the possibilities and potentials of which will be interestingly tested and used in years to come. Hypermedia and related technologies provide important possibilities for enhancing the learning, experience, and quality of life for challenged individuals.

8

CONCLUSION

Computer-based adaptive technology first became a practical possibility with the introduction of inexpensive microcomputers during the late 1970s. The field has rapidly developed over the past ten or fifteen years, moving from microcomputers with only keyboard input and very limited memory, to systems with massive memory and highly sophisticated input and output devices. How much the technology has changed is indicated by the fact that the internal memory of the machines that were being used in the early 1980s was thirty-two or sixty-four kilobytes. Today, inexpensive notebook computers typically have a minimum of one megabyte, while the desktop computer on which this chapter is being written is eight megabytes, or approximately 125 times greater than the widely used sixty-four-kilobyte machines of a decade ago.

As we advance into the final years of the decade and the beginning of the new millennium, computers will not only become significantly larger and faster, but new software and interface systems will greatly expand the potential for using computers for individuals with special needs.

In this book, we have tried to suggest some of the directions that might be taken in the near future. For example, we are just beginning to experiment with using virtual reality techniques to enable people in the physical and cognitive domains. Similarly, the use of hypermedia systems to augment how we think and function, is only just beginning to be understood.

Clearly, technology provides both solutions and obstacles for individuals with disabilities. In a culture that depends heavily on telephones for communication, a deaf individual is at a decided disadvantage unless the technology (i.e., the telephone) is adapted to his or her needs. Here lies the critical problem for those interested in the field of adaptive technology—that is how to not only adapt technology to the needs of special populations, but how to get it into their hands so that they can use it on a practical basis.

Such questions raise issues related to affordability, training, and effective interface design. These are all issues which we have attempted to address in the preceding chapters of this work. Yet perhaps an even larger issue subsumes these areas—that is how to effectively train people to use these new technologies. As demonstrated in our case studies, the implementation and use of adaptive technology is a process that has been significantly limited by the lack of appropriate training at a number of levels. In the case of Carrie Seigenthaler, for example, the failure of her employers to provide her with minimal adaptive equipment and train her in its use determined whether or not she would succeed in her work. With Mike Morgan, it is clear that considerable training and support needs to be provided not just for his teachers, but also for his parents and probably even for his siblings.

Conditions necessary for the acceptance and use of adaptive technology include increasing awareness of what possibilities are available, making new equipment and programs more affordable, and providing individuals with disabilities the necessary support to take full advantage of the technology that is available to them. An individual with communication problems, for example, needs to be made fully aware of what types of technology are on the market for his or her particular problem, must have the financial resources to purchase it, and needs thorough quality training and support to be able to take full advantage of the technology's capabilities. To illustrate this last point: it is useless for an individual to have access to a printer that uses large type fonts if the user does not know how to, or does not have somebody who can help him or her, get access to them. It is not enough just to have the technology—one must also know how to use it.

In our interview with Carol Farrell, a seasoned professional and special educator with extensive experience in the use of adaptive technology, she explained that:

Technology is overwhelming even for me. And I have been working with these devices since they first came out. There are so many different devices, and so many different levels and upgrades for each one. For example, one teacher has three different versions of the Adaptive Firmware Card in her computers. Each of these cards requires a different set of directions to operate.

If using adaptive technology is difficult for professionals such as Carol to use, then it is even more of a problem for parents and other non-professionals who have little experience with computers or other types of technology. As Carol explains:

There are some parents who are capable of accepting technology and incorporating it into their children's lives, but many of the parents of children with disabilities can barely take care of themselves. Technology just isn't going to fit into their lives. People who don't even own cars can't deal with technology. These families are just overwhelmed by life itself.

Parents, teachers, and those who are in teacher preparation programs need to be much more systematically introduced to the possibilities and limitations provided by adaptive technology. This is a difficult problem in a number of regards. Teachers in the field who are not computer-literate need to become skilled in the possibilities provided by the new technology. This is often hard to accomplish in light of limited budgets and time, and the fact that new innovations are constantly changing and redefining the field. One need only look at the technology that was widely in use four or five years ago to realize the extent to which one must constantly work to keep up in the area. While this is difficult even for the specialist, it is even more of a problem for teachers who have concerns other than just technology for their students with special needs.

However, it should also be noted that adaptive technology can greatly facilitate the regular classroom teacher's work with mainstreamed children with special needs. In their interviews with us, both Beth Sanders and Carol Farrell commented that the children with whom they worked were not always making use of adaptive technology systems in their regular classrooms because their regular teachers did not have the necessary skill or training to work well with their equipment. These arguments also apply to parents who, like teachers, need to be introduced and supported in the use of new technology.

This raises a basic problem, which becomes more of an issue as we increasingly use adaptive technology with children who have special needs. As technology becomes more complex and sophisticated, the demands of training and support increase as well. In this context, it is absolutely crucial that as new systems are designed they include easily used interfaces, incorporate in useful ways existing and familiar technologies, and in general make the process of working in the field as clear and as uncomplicated as possible. The regular classroom teacher simply does not have the time to become an expert in computer use and in sub-systems involving adaptive technology. Such technologies must be as clear and straightforward in their use as possible, if they are to be used and incorporated into the regular classroom.

Finally, as a culture, we need to realize that the use of adaptive technology is not just simply a technical question, but one involving deeper and more profound questions of equity. What obligations do we have as a society to provide enabling technologies to those who have disabilities? Who should have access to such services? At what level? Where should funding come from?

Other questions arise as well. At what point does the use of adaptive technology begin to interfere with what it means to be human? What about the use of a cochlear implant for a child who is deaf? If parents object to the use of technology with their child, do government agencies have the right to intervene on behalf of the child? Carol Farrell raised this question when she explained that:

> Some parents are not accepting of technology. When electric typewriters became available, some parents were very reluctant to give up on handwriting. They felt that if students were allowed to use the typewriter, they would never learn to write.

These were students who probably would never be able to write because of their disabilities. The same is true for communication devices. Some parents see the communication device as a crutch which will prevent their child from even trying to speak. Once again these children would most likely never be able to speak. Some parents would rather not have their children speak at all than use communication devices. They say that it's just not normal.

We feel strongly that an essential part of being human involves being able to communicate. Not making such technologies available to children with disabilities is in most instances a serious mistake.

A promising recent development has been the Americans with Disabilities Act, which was passed by Congress in July of 1990. Under this law, individuals with disabilities are provided protection in sectors of private employment, all public services, public accommodations, transportation, and telecommunication. As the law becomes more fully implemented, individuals with disabilities will be able to demand greater access and support for systems, based on adaptive technology, that provide them the opportunity to function as normally as possible.

In final conclusion, adaptive technology's potential to empower individuals with disabilities is clear. However, its use requires careful consideration and reflection on the part of families, educators, counselors, and therapists. It is hoped that the preceding pages have provided a useful introduction to the promises and limitations inherent in this important, rapidly evolving, and fascinating field.

APPENDIX A

MANUFACTURERS AND DISTRIBUTORS

ACS Technologies
1400 Lee Drive
Coraopolis, PA 15108

Communication devices,
including RealVoice,
EvalPac, and SpeechPac

ADAMLAB
Wayne County Regional
  Educational Service Agency
33500 Van Born Road
Wayne, MI 48184

Wolf communication device

AI Squared
P. O. Box 669
Manchester Center, VT 05255

Text magnification software

Animated Voice Corporation
P. O. Box 819
San Marcos, CA 92069

Ani-Vox speech system

Apple Computer, Inc.
20525 Mariani Avenue
Cupertino, CA 95014

HyperCard authoring system

Ariel Corporation
433 River Road
Highland Park, NJ 08904

SpeechStation

Artic Technologies
55 Park Street
Troy, MI 48083

Computer access for visually
  impaired

Articulate Systems, Inc. 600 West Cummings Park Woburn, MA 01801	Voice Navigator voice input device
Asymetrix Corporation 110–110th Avenue, NE Bellevue, WA 98007	Toolbook authoring system
Autodesk, Inc. P. O. Box 84883 Seattle, WA 98124	Cyberspace
Baylor Biomedical Services 2625 Elm Street Dallas, TX 75226	Altkey keyboard emulator
Berkeley Systems 2095 Rose Street Berkeley, CA 94709	OutSPOKEN GUI access
Blazie Engineering 105 East Jarrettsville Road Forest Hill, MD 21050	Braille products
BrainTrain 727 Twin Ridge Lane Richmond, VA 23235	Software
Broderbund Software, Inc. P. O. Box 6130 Novato, CA 94948	Software
Creative Switch Industries P. O. Box 5256 DesMoines, IA 50306	Switches
Crestwood Company 6625 North Sidney Place Milwaukee, WI 53209	Communication aids

CUE SoftSwap
4655 Old Ironsides Drive
Santa Clara, CA 95052

Hypermedia authoring
 software

Davidson & Associates, Inc.
P. O. Box 2961
Torrance, CA 90509

Software

Disabled Programmers, Inc.
151 Martinvale Lane
San Jose, CA 95119

ESL Tutor for hearing
 impaired

Don Johnston, Inc.
1000 N. Rand Road
Wauconda, IL 60084-0639

Computer access, including
 Adaptive Firmware Card
 and Ke:nx

Dragon Systems, Inc.
320 Nevada Street
Newton, MA 02160

DragonDictate

Dunamis, Inc.
3620 Highway 317
Suwanee, GA 30174

PowerPad

Echo Speech Corporation
6460 Via Real
Carpenteria, CA 93013

Speech synthesizer

Edmark Corporation
P. O. Box 3218
Redmond, WA 980732

TouchWindow and software

Exceptional Children's Software
P. O. Box 487
Hays, KS 67601

Software

EyeMouse
Professor Glenn Myers
Dept. of Biomedical Engineering
University of Iowa
Iowa City, IO 52242

EyeMouse

First Byte   Software
19840 Pioneer Avenue
Torrance, CA 90503

Franklin   Communication devices
122 Burrs Road
Mt. Holly, NJ 08060

Hartley, Inc.   Software
3001 Coolidge Road
East Lansing, MI 48823

Health Care Keyboard Co., Inc.   Comfort Keyboard
N82 W15340 Appleton Avenue
Menomonee Falls, WI 53051

IBM: Eduquest   AccessDos, Linkway,
P. O. Box 1328   THINKable Phone
Boca Raton, FL 33432   Communicator, Screen
                                        Reader, SpeechViewer,
                                        VoiceType

Infogrip, Inc.   BAT
5800 One Perkins Place
Baton Rouge, LA 70808

Innocomp   Augmentative
26210 Emery Road   communication products
Warrensville Heights, OH 44139

IntelliTools   Unicorn keyboard and
5221 Central Avenue   IntelliKeys
Richmond, CA 94804

Interactive Learning Materials   Write This Way software
1109 East Sunnyslope Street
Petaluma, CA 94952

In Touch Systems   Magic Wand Keyboard
11 Westview Road
Spring Valley, NY 10977

Koala Acquisitions, Inc.   Koala Pad
16055 Caputo Drive
Morgan Hill, CA 95037

Kurzweil Computer Products   Products for visually
411 Waverly Oaks Road   impaired, including
Waltham, MA 02154   VOICE

Laureate Learning Systems   Software, including First
110 East Spring Street   Verbs, First Categories,
Winnooski, VT 05404   Words and Concepts,
                                    and Creature Antics

Lawrence Productions, Inc.   Software
1800 South 35th Street
Galesburg, MI 49053

LC Technologies, Inc.   Eyegaze Computer System
9455 Silver King Street
Fairfax, VA 22031

Lehigh Valley Microcomputer   Public domain software
    Project
P. O. Box 333
Kulpsville, PA 19443

Leithauser Research   No-Keys software
4649 Van Kleeck Drive
New Smyrna Beach, FL 32169

Marblesoft   Software
12301 Central Avenue N.E.
Blaine, MN 55434

Matias Corporation   Half-QWERTY keyboard
178 Thistledown Boulevard
Rexdale, Ontario, Canada M9V 1K1

McIntyre Computer Systems   WordWriter and LipStick
22809 Shagbark
Birmingham, MI 48025

MECC   Software
6160 Summit Drive North
St. Paul, MN 55430

Microsystems Software, Inc.   HandiKEY on-screen
600 Worcester Road   keyboard
Framingham, MA 01701

Milliken Publishing Company   Software
1100 Research Boulevard
P. O. Box 21579
St. Louis, MO 63132

Mindplay   Software
P. O. Box 36491
Tuscon, AZ 85740

Mindscape, Inc.   Software
1345 Diversity Parkway
Chicago, IL 60614

National Geographic   Software
Educational Services
17th and M Streets, NW
Washington, DC 20036

Optimum Resources, Inc.   Software
10 Station Place
Norfolk, CT 06058

Parallel Systems, Inc.   Keasyboard
P. O. Box 58435
Vancouver, British Columbia
Canada V6P6K2

PEAL Software   Software, including
P. O. Box 8188   KeyTalk, Exploratory
Calabasas, CA 91372   Play, and
                                           Representational Play

Pelican Software, Inc.   Software
768 Farmington Avenue
Farmington, CT 06032

Prentke Romich   Switches and
1022 Heyl Road   communication devices,
Wooster, OH 44691   including Light Talker
                                             and Touch Talker

R. J. Cooper & Associates   Adaptive hardware and
24843 Del Prado   software
Dana Point, CA 92629

Robotic Assistance Corporation   Robotics
c/o Peter Movsesian
P. O. Box 5278
Santa Ana, CA 92704

Scholastic, Inc.   Software
2931 East McCarty Street
Jefferson City, MO 65102

Sentient Systems Technology   Dynavox and other
2100 Wharton Street   communication aids
Pittsburgh, PA 15203

Street Electronics   Speech synthesizer
1140 Mark Avenue
Carpenteria, CA 93013

Sunburst Communications   Muppet Learning Keys and
39 Washington Avenue   software
Pleasantville, NY 10570

Syntha-voice Computer, Inc.   Slimware Window Bridge
800 Queenston Road
Stone Creek, ON Canada L8G 1A7

Tash   Mini keyboards, switches,
Unit 1, 91 Station Street   etc.
Ajax, Ontario, Canada L1S 3H2

TeleSensory 455 North Bernardo Avenue Mountain View, CA 94043	Products for visually impaired including BrailleMate and outSPOKEN speech output
Tom Snyder Productions 80 Coolidge Hill Road Watertown, MA 02172	Software
Toys for Special Children 385 Warburton Avenue Hastings-on-Hudson, NY 10706	Switches and communication devices
UCLA/LAUSD Microcomputer Project c/o UCLA Intervention Program 1000 Veteran Avenue 23-10 Rehab Los Angeles, CA 90024	Software
Universal Robot Systems c/o Thomas Carroll 7025 El Paseo Street Long Beach, CA 90815	Robotics
Visage, Inc. 1881 Worcester Road Framingham, MA 01701	TouchMate (touch input)
Voyager Company 1351 Pacific Coast Highway Santa Monica, CA 90401	Videodiscs and software
Xerox Imaging Systems 9 Centenial Drive Peabody, MA 01960	Kurzweil Reader, The Reading Edge, and The Reading Tutor
Zygo Industries P. O. Box 1008 Portland, OR 97207-1008	Communication devices

APPENDIX B

INFORMATION SERVICES AND DATA BASES

CompuServe
P. O. Box 20212
Columbus, OH 43220
1-800-848-8199

GEnie
General Electric Information Services
401 N. Washington Street
Rockville, MD 20850
1-800-638-9636

Prodigy
Prodigy Services Company
445 Hamilton Avenue
White Plains, NY 10615

SpecialNet
GTE Educational Services
8505 Freeport Parkway, Suite 600
Irving TX 75063
1-800-634-5644

Trace Research and Development Center
1500 Highland Avenue
University of Wisconsin
Madison, WI 53706

APPENDIX C

ORGANIZATIONS INVOLVED WITH ADAPTIVE TECHNOLOGY

ABLEDATA
National Rehabilitation Information Center
Catholic University
4407 Eighth Street NE
Washington, DC 20017

ACTT (Activating Children Through Technology)
c/o Western Illinois University
27 Horrabin Hall
Macomb, IL 61455

Alexander Graham Bell Association
3417 Volta Place N.W.
Washington, D.C. 20007

American Foundation for the Blind
15 West 16th Street
New York, NY 10011

American Printing House for the Blind
1839 Frankfort Avenue
Louisville, KY 40206

American Speech-Language-Hearing Association
10801 Rockville Pike
Rockville, MD 20852

Apple Special Education Division
Apple Computer
20525 S. 36M
Cupertino, CA 95014

Association for Special Education Technology
P. O. Box 152
Allen, TX 75002-0152

Center for Special Education Technology
Council for Exceptional Children
1920 Association Drive
Reston, VA 22091-1589

Closing the Gap
P. O. Box 68
Henderson, MN 56044

Colorado Easter Seal Society
Center for Adapted Technology
5755 West Alameda
Lakewood, CO 80226

Computer Users in Speech and Hearing
CUSH Business Office
P. O. Box 2160
Hudson, OH 44236

Council for Exceptional Children
1920 Association Drive
Reston, VA 22091

IBM/Special Needs Exchange
c/o LINC Resources
P. O. Box 434
Pawtucket, RI 02862

IBM National Support Center for Persons with Disabilities
P. O. Box 2150
Atlanta, GA 30055

Information Center for Special Education Media and Materials
c/o LINC Resources
4820 Indianola Avenue
Columbus, OH 43214

International Society for Augmentative and Alternative Communication
P. O. Box 1762, Station R
Toronto, ON, Canada M4G 4A3

International Society for Technology in Education
University of Oregon
1787 Agate Street
Eugene, OR 97403-9905

National Braille Press
88 St. Stephen Street
Boston, MA 02115

National Easter Seal Society
70 East Lake Street
Chicago, IL 60601

National Lekotek Center
2100 Ridge Avenue
Evanston, IL 60204

Resources for Rehabilitation
33 Bedford Street, Suite 19A
Lexington, MA 02173

Technology and Media Division
Council for Exceptional Children
1920 Association Drive
Reston, VA 22091-1589

UCLA Intervention Program for Handicapped Children
1000 Veteran Avenue
Los Angeles, CA 90024

United Cerebral Palsy Association
66 East 34th Street
New York, NY 10016

NOTES

CHAPTER 1. INTRODUCTION

1. Glenn Rifkin, "A Wider Work Force by Computer," *The New York Times*, Sunday December 16, 1990, Section F, p. 11.

2. John O. Green, "New Ways for Special Ed Kids to Communicate," *Classroom Computer Learning*, October 1984. pp. 26 and 29.

3. Ann Blackman, "Machines that Work Miracles," *Time*, February 18, 1991, pp. 70.

4. *Ibid.*, p. 71.

5. Eugene F. Provenzo, Jr., *Beyond the Gutenberg Galaxy: Microcomputers and the Emergence of Post-Typographic Culture* (New York: Teachers College Press, 1986).

6. *Ibid.*, p. 4.

7. Douglas Englebart, "A Conceptual Framework for the Augmentation of Man's Intellect." In P. W. Howerton and D. C. Weeks, *Vistas in Information Handling: Vol. 1. The Augmentation of Man's Intellect by Machine.* (Washington, D.C.: Spartan Books, 1963), pp. 1–29.

8. *Ibid.*, p. 1.

9. *Ibid.*, p. 3.

10. *Ibid.*

11. William Gibson's novels describing cyberspace include *Neuromancer* (New York: Ace Books, 1984); *Count Zero* (New York: Ace Books, 1986); and *Mona Lisa Overdrive* (New York: Bantam, 1989). Vernor Vinge describes cyberspace in his collection of short stories entitled *True Names...and Other Dangers* (New York: Baen Publishing, 1987).

12. Norbert Wiener, *The Human Use of Human Beings: Cybernetics and Society* (New York; Avon Books, 1967), pp. 24–25.

13. Ted Nelson, *Computer Lib* (Redmond, WA: Microsoft Press, 1987), p. 149.

14. C. A. Bowers, *The Cultural Dimensions of Educational Computing: Understanding the Non-Neutrality of Technology* (New York: Teachers College Press, 1980), p. 24.

15. *Ibid.*

16. *Ibid.*, p. 27.

17. *Ibid.*, pp. 32–33.

18. For background on virtual reality as a technology and its cultural implications see Howard Rheingold *Virtual Reality* (New York: Summit Books, 1991).

19. Steven Levy, "Brave New World," *Rolling Stone*, June 14, 1990, p. 92.

20. Bob Pointing, "Virtual Reality System Readied," *Infoworld*, July 24, 1989, pp. 17 and 22. Cyberspace's headset display consists of wide angle optics and two-color LCD displays mounted inside the frame of a scuba diving mask. A device called an Isotrak is mounted on the headset and sends the position and orientation of the headset to the computer. The Cyberspace software uses position information to provide separate views of the 3-D scene for each eye.

The first head-mounted, three-dimensional display, or virtual reality interface, was built in 1968 and used two small CRT displays mounted in a helmet that was attached to the ceiling by a mechanical shaft that measured head movement. In 1985 NASA developed a head-mounted screen using LCD screens and the Isotrak device to measure the position and orientation of the helmet. The Isotrak device allowed its user to function without being attached to a mechanical shaft that limits one's natural movement.

21. Hans Moravec, *Mind Children* (Cambridge: Harvard University Press, 1989).

CHAPTER 2. COMPUTERS AND SPECIAL NEEDS

1. Jackie Fox, "Unlocking the Door: PCs and People With Disabilities," *PCToday*, Vol 8, March 1991, p. 45.

2. Lawrence Cremin, *The Genius of American Education* (New York: Vantage Books, 1965), pp. 37–38.

3. Anthony Chandor with John Graham and Robin Williamson, *The Penguin Dictionary of Computers*, (New York: Penguin Books, 1982), p. 89.

4. Royal Van Horn, *Advanced Technology in Education*. (Belmont, California: Brooks/Cole Pub Co., 1991), p. 24.

5. Gwen C. Nugent, "The Videodisc: A New Tool in Teaching the Handicapped," *Journal of Special Education Technology*, Vol. III, no. 3, Spring 1980, p. 68.

6. William Hawkins, "CD Libraries: New Power for Home PCS," *Popular Science*, May 1990, p. 75, and Penelope Semrau and Barbara Boyer, *Using Interactive Video in Education* (Boston: Allyn and Bacon, 1994), pp. 35–36.

7. *Ibid.*, pp. 40–42.

8. Van Horn, pp. 67–73.

9. Hans Moravec, *Mind Children: The Future of Robot and Human Intelligence* (Cambridge: Harvard University Press, 1988).

10. Robert Taylor, *The Computer in the School: Tutor, Tool, Tutee* (Santa Cruz, California: Mitchell Publishing Co., 1980).

11. Seymour Papert, *Mindstorms: Children, Computers and Powerful Ideas* (New York: Basic Books, 1980).

12. Cleborne D. Maddux, "Issues and Concerns in Special Education Microcomputing," *Computers in the Schools*, Vol. 3 no. 3–4, Fall-Winter 1986, p. 3.

13. *Ibid.*, p. 3.

14. Edward J. Cain, "The Role of the Computer in Special Education: Some Philosophical Considerations," *The Pointer*, Winter 1984, pp. 6–7.

15. Witold Rybczynski, *Taming the Tiger: The Struggle to Control Technology* (New York: Penguin Books, 1985), pp. 3–4.

CHAPTER 3. INPUT ANDOUTPUT DEVICES

1. Michael Chen and Frank Leahy, "A Design for Supporting New Input Devices," in Brenda Laurel, editor, *The Art of Human-Computer Interface Design* (Reading, MA: Addison-Wesley Publishing Company, 1990), p. 300. For other discussions of interface issues see the various essays included in this work.

2. Glenn Myers, "The EyeMouse," *Zenith Data Systems: Supplement to T.H.E. Journal*, Vol. 19, no. 6, January 1992, pp. 13–15.

CHAPTER 4. ADAPTIVE TECHNOLOGY AND
THE PHYSICALLY AND VISUALLY IMPAIRED

1. William Heward and Michael Orlansky, *Exceptional Children* (New York: Macmillan, 1992), pp. 377–378.

2. A. L. Corn, "Instruction in the Use of Vision for Children and Adults with Low Vision: A Proposed Program Model," *RE:view*, Vol. 21 1989, p. 28.

3. Barbara T. Mates, "CD-ROM: A New Light for the Blind and Visually Impaired" *Computers in Libraries*, March 1990, pp. 17–20.

CHAPTER 5. ADAPTIVE TECHNOLOGY AND
THE SPEECH AND HEARING IMPAIRED

1. "Advanced computer speech trainer unveiled at Lexington center," Press release, Matushita Electrical Industrial Company (Panasonic) New York, January 19, 1989. 5 pages.

2. Dan Littman and Tom Moran, "Macworld News," *Macworld*, March 1991, pp. 99–100.

3. Jorge Ortega, "DOE Sponsored Instructional Technology Products for Special Students," *Florida Technology in Education Quarterly*, Vol 3 no. 2, Winter 1991, pp. 7–8.

4. Mary Wilson, *Sequential Software for Language Development* (Winooski, Vermont: Laureate Learning Systems, 1991).

5. "IBM System Helps Hearing, Speech-Impaired," *Electronic Learning*, February 1990, p. 43.

6. Laura Meyers, "Teaching Language," *The Exceptional Parent*, November 1986, pp. 20–23.

7. Jeffrey Braden and Steven Shaw, "Computer Assisted Instruction with Young Children: Panacea, Placebo or Poison?" *American Annals of the Deaf*, July 1987, pp. 189–193.

8. Lisa O'Connor and Teris Schery, "A Comparison of Microcomputer-aided and Traditional Language Therapy for Developing Communication Skills in Nonoral Toddlers," *Journal of Speech and Hearing Disorders*, Vol. 51, November 1986, pp. 356–361.

9. Philip Prinz and Keith Nelson, "Acquisition of Writing and Reading Skills by Deaf Children Using the Microcomputer," *Applied Psycholinguistics*, Vol. 6, 1985, pp. 283–306.

CHAPTER 6. ADAPTIVE TECHNOLOGY AND
THE COGNITIVELY IMPAIRED

1. Janet Learner, *Learning Disabilities*, fifth edition (New Jersey: Houghton Mifflin Company, 1988), p. 7.

2. *Ibid.*, p. 7.

3. Charles MacArthur, Jacqueline Haynes, David Malouf, Karen Harris, Maria Owings, "Computer Assisted Instruction with Learning Disabled Students: Achievement, Engagement, and Other Factors that Influence Achievement," *Journal of Educational Computing Research*, Vol. 6 no. 3 1990, pp. 311–328.

4. Council for Exceptional Children, "Learning Disabilities," *Tech Use Guide: Using Computer Technology* (Reston, Virginia: Center for Special Education Technology, 1989).

5. M. Cochran-Smith, "Word Processing and Writing in Elementary Classrooms: A Critical Review of Related Literature," *Review of Educational Research*, Vol. 61, 1991, pp. 107–155.

6. Sheila Iseman, "The Laptop Computer: A Bridge to Literacy for Students with Learning Disabilities," *Closing the Gap*, Vol. 12, no. 3, Aug/Sept 1993, pp. 10–11, 22.

7. H. J. Grossman, Editor, *Classification in Mental Retardation* (Washington, D.C.: American Association on Mental Deficiency, 1983), p. 11.

8. *Ibid.*

9. William Heward and Michael Orlansky, *Exceptional Children* Fourth edition (New York: Macmillan, 1992), 104.

10. Robert W. White, "Motivation reconsidered: The concept of competence." In M. Almy (Ed.). *Early Childhood Play: Selected Readings Related to Cognition and Motivation.* (New York: Simon and Schuster, 1968).

11. E. Nelson, "Learned helplessness and children's achievement." In S. Moore & K. Kolb (Eds.). *Reviews of Research for Practitioners and Parents.* (Minneapolis: Center for Early Education and Development, University of Minnesota, 1987).

CHAPTER 7. HYPERMEDIA AND INDIVIDUALS WITH SPECIAL NEEDS

1. Theodor Holm Nelson, *Literary Machines*, Edition 87.1 (The Report On, And Of, Project Xanadu Concerning Word Processing, Electronic Publishing, Hypertext, Thinkertoys, Tomorrow's Intellectual Revolution, And Certain Other Topics Including Knowledge, Education and Freedom) (Bellevue, Washington: Microsoft Press, 1987), p. o/2.

2. *Ibid.*

3. Jeff Conklin, "Hypertext: An Introduction and Survey," *Computer*, Vol. 20, No. 9, p. 17.

INDEX